T0326315

# Cambridge Elements ≡

Elements in Criminology
edited by
David Weisburd
*George Mason University, Virginia*
*Hebrew University of Jerusalem*

# THE FUTURE OF THE CRIMINOLOGY OF PLACE

## *New Directions for Research and Practice*

David Weisburd
*George Mason University, Virginia*
*Hebrew University of Jerusalem*

Barak Ariel
*Hebrew University of Jerusalem*
*University of Cambridge*

Anthony A. Braga
*University of Pennsylvania*

John Eck
*University of Cincinnati*

Charlotte Gill
*George Mason University*

Elizabeth Groff
*National Institute of Justice*

Clair V. Uding
*University of Wyoming*

Amarat Zaatut
*Temple University*

CAMBRIDGE
UNIVERSITY PRESS

Shaftesbury Road, Cambridge CB2 8EA, United Kingdom

One Liberty Plaza, 20th Floor, New York, NY 10006, USA

477 Williamstown Road, Port Melbourne, VIC 3207, Australia

314–321, 3rd Floor, Plot 3, Splendor Forum, Jasola District Centre,
New Delhi – 110025, India

103 Penang Road, #05–06/07, Visioncrest Commercial, Singapore 238467

Cambridge University Press is part of Cambridge University Press & Assessment,
a department of the University of Cambridge.

We share the University's mission to contribute to society through the pursuit of
education, learning and research at the highest international levels of excellence.

www.cambridge.org
Information on this title: www.cambridge.org/9781009590983

DOI: 10.1017/9781009590952

First published 2024

*A catalogue record for this publication is available from the British Library*

ISBN 978-1-009-59098-3 Hardback
ISBN 978-1-009-59097-6 Paperback
ISSN 2633-3341 (online)
ISSN 2633-3333 (print)

# The Future of the Criminology of Place

## New Directions for Research and Practice

Elements in Criminology

DOI: 10.1017/9781009590952
First published online: December 2024

David Weisburd
*George Mason University, Virginia*
*Hebrew University of Jerusalem*

Barak Ariel
*Hebrew University of Jerusalem*
*University of Cambridge*

Anthony A. Braga
*University of Pennsylvania*

John Eck
*University of Cincinnati*

Charlotte Gill
*George Mason University*

Elizabeth Groff
*National Institute of Justice*

Clair V. Uding
*University of Wyoming*

Amarat Zaatut
*Temple University*

**Author for correspondence:** David Weisburd, david.weisburd@mail.huji.ac.il

**Abstract:** Microgeographic units of analysis have moved to the center of criminological inquiry. This Element brings together leading crime-and-place scholars to identify promising areas for future study. Section 1 introduces the Element and the importance of focusing on the future of studies of crime and place. Section 2 examines the development of hot-spots policing and the importance of focusing on its impact on communities. It also looks at how "pracademics" can advance the science and practice of place-based policing. Section 3 focuses on place managers as prevention agents and examines how city government can influence crime at place. Section 4 contends that rural communities need to become a key focus of crime-and-place scholarship, emphasizes the importance of the connection of health, crime, and place, and argues for the importance of expanding the methodological tools of crime and place to include careful ethnographic and qualitative research.

**Keywords:** crime and place, crime concentration, policing, public health, research methods

ISBNs: 9781009590983 (HB), 9781009590976 (PB), 9781009590952 (OC)
ISSNs: 2633-3341 (online), 2633-3333 (print)

# Contents

## 1 Introduction

The study of crime at microgeographic units of analysis began to interest criminologists in the late 1980s (Evans & Herbert, 1989; Felson, 1987; Pierce et al., 1988; Sherman et al., 1989; Weisburd & Green, 1994; Weisburd et al., 1992). In 1989, in *Criminology*, Lawrence Sherman, Patrick Gartin, and Michael Buerger coined the term *criminology of place* to describe this new area of study (Sherman et al., 1989). The criminology of place (see also Weisburd et al., 2012) or *crime and place* (see Eck & Weisburd, 1995) pushes us to examine very small geographic areas within cities, often as small as addresses or street segments (a street from intersection to intersection), and not larger than small clusters of such units, for their contribution to the crime problem. It pushes us to ask why crime occurs at specific places.

This focus is critically important since it suggests a major turning point in how criminologists understand crime. Just a generation ago, criminology was primarily concerned with "why criminals commit crime." This was seen not only as the primary basic research question for criminology but also as the key approach to doing something about the crime problem. While "who done it" remains a dominant area of research in criminology (Eck & Eck, 2012; Weisburd, 2015), "where done it" has also moved to the center of criminological inquiry. Indeed, in terms of crime prevention, focus on *where* crime occurs has perhaps become the dominant focus of research and theory. Situational crime prevention (Clarke, 1980, 1983), routine activity theory (Cohen & Felson, 1979), and crime pattern theory (Brantingham & Brantingham, 1993; Brantingham et al., 2017) are now key theoretical perspectives in criminology, and all look at the specific places where crime occurs as a crucial part of the crime prevention equation.

We now have a large and strong body of evidence that shows that crime is extremely concentrated in small places (Lee et al., 2017; Weisburd, 2015; Weisburd et al., 2024), that this concentration is often stable across time (Weisburd et al., 2004, 2012; also see Andresen et al., 2017a, 2017b; Harinam et al., 2022; Wheeler et al., 2016), and that crime hot spots are not bad neighborhoods but rather street segments, street corners, or even single addresses (or small clusters of these units) that are driving the crime rates for larger areas (Weisburd et al., 2012, 2016a). These findings have been reinforced by a large number of crime prevention studies that show that when police or other resources are focused at microgeographic hot spots they will be effective in reducing crime problems (Braga & Weisburd, 2022; Braga et al., 2019). It is fair to say today that, in contrast to a generation ago, just showing that crime is concentrated or that hot-spots approaches are effective is not enough to provide important new knowledge about crime and place.

So what are key areas for future study in this field? That is the focus of this Element, which brings together leading crime-and-place scholars to identify important and promising avenues for advancing the criminology of place over the next decade. We begin with Section 2.1 by Anthony A. Braga, on the future of hot-spots policing research. Policing has been the context in which crime and place has had perhaps the most influence in altering traditional crime prevention. For example, there are now more than sixty studies that evaluate hot-spots policing programs, far outnumbering research in other areas of policing. And there is a strong consensus that hot-spots policing works, reinforced both by Campbell Collaboration systematic reviews (Braga & Weisburd, 2022; Braga et al., 2019) and by narrative reviews by the National Academies of Science (Skogan & Frydl, 2004; Weisburd & Majmundar, 2018). Following on from this section, we examine more directly what is necessary in the future for place-based policing to become a routinized part of the toolbox of proactive policing in police agencies. In Section 2.2 Barak Ariel reports on his experiences with pracademics and how the pracademic can both improve the nature of hot-spots policing research and influence the utility of that research in policing. After these sections, we turn to place managers. The question asked here is how we can follow upon the law of crime concentration not only with innovations in policing but with innovations in how we utilize other managers of places. In Section 3.1 John Eck argues that place managers other than the police should play a key role in future research and practice in crime prevention. Then, regarding prevention approaches, in Section 3.2 Elizabeth Groff focuses on how local government can play a key role in advancing the study of both crime and place, and crime prevention.

Having focused on multiple directions in prevention research and practice, we turn to a series of questions about expanding the focus of crime-and-place research in terms of the jurisdictions that are studied, the outcomes that are examined, and the methods that are used to explore research questions. First, in Section 4.1 Charlotte Gill notes the lack of research on rural jurisdictions, despite the fact that most places and most police agencies fall under this rubric. Using evidence on crime concentrations in a research program in a rural jurisdiction, she argues that a comprehensive science of crime and place must include more focus on rural jurisdictions. In Section 4.2 Clair V. Uding exam ines the relationship between crime hot spots and health outcomes. Using examples from a large longitudinal study of crime hot spots in Baltimore, Maryland, she illustrates why mental health outcomes should become a key concern for crime-and-place studies. Finally, in Section 4.3 Amarat Zaatut explores the importance of more qualitative research in crime-and-place studies. Noting that there has been little qualitative study in the criminology of place, she goes on to illustrate how it can be useful and why it should be a key direction for future basic research.

## 2 Prevention and Policing

### 2.1 Hot-Spots Policing Research: Taking Stock of Existing Knowledge and Hypothesizing Future Directions

Hot-spots policing has become a very popular way for police departments to prevent crime (see, e.g., Police Executive Research Forum, 2008; Reaves, 2010).[1] Many police departments report having the capability to manage and analyze crime data in sophisticated ways and, through management innovations such as CompStat, hold officers accountable for implementing problem-solving strategies to control crime at hot spots (Weisburd et al., 2003). In the words of then-New York City Police Department (NYPD) deputy commissioner Jack Maple, "the main principle of deployment can be expressed in one sentence: 'Map the crime and put the cops where the dots are.' Or, more succinctly: 'Put cops on dots'" (Maple, 1999: 128). These practical changes to police strategy were occurring in the context of theoretical innovations recognizing that the bulk of the crime problem occurs at a small number of specific places such as addresses, intersection areas, and block faces (Sherman et al., 1989; Weisburd et al., 1992), and through rigorous field tests to determine whether the application of police intervention at very small geographic units of analysis – popularly known as "hot-spots policing" – reduced crime (Braga et al., 1999; Sherman & Weisburd, 1995; Weisburd & Green, 1995).

Hot-spots policing research questions posed by scholars evolved considerably over the last decades of the twentieth century and the first decades of the twenty-first century. First, researchers sought to determine whether putting "cops on dots" generated crime control gains using rigorous randomized controlled trials and quasi-experimental designs (e.g., see Sherman & Rogan, 1995; Sherman & Weisburd, 1995). Second, studies sought to determine whether the type of hot-spots policing program implemented could produce stronger (or weaker) crime control gains. More recently, persistent questions of police legitimacy stemming from large-scale racial justice protests raised by tragic events such as the 2014 police shooting of Michael Brown in Ferguson, Missouri and the more recent 2020 murder of George Floyd at the hands of a Minneapolis police officer have led to research on unintended harms generated

---

[1] Section 2.1 was drafted by Anthony A. Braga.

by overly aggressive policing strategies. This section summarizes the existing scientific evidence supporting hot-spots policing and the efficacy of differing police strategies used to reduce crime at hot spots. It then suggests that the next generation of research will be focused on reducing unintended harms of law enforcement while maintaining proactivity in hot spots and maximizing police legitimacy.

### 2.1.1 Evaluating Crime Prevention Benefits

Starting in the late 1980s, a collaboration between Lawrence Sherman and David Weisburd led to the development of the first randomized controlled trial that explicitly tested the effects of hot-spots policing on crime (Sherman & Weisburd, 1995). Data collected as part of a previous problem-oriented policing study in Minneapolis, Minnesota showed that 50 percent of citizen calls for service occurred at only 3.5 percent of the city's street addresses (Sherman et al., 1989). In turn, Weisburd, in a community policing study in the 72nd precinct in New York City, had just observed tremendous concentration of crime on specific streets within the beats the police patrolled (see Gladwell, 2019: 280–283). Sherman and Weisburd (1995) considered how the implications of these findings impacted conclusions reached about the ineffectiveness of police patrol by the landmark Kansas City Preventive Patrol Experiment (Kelling et al., 1974). They reasoned that spreading police patrol resources evenly across large areas, such as police districts, made little sense if crime was clustered at a few geographically small "hot-spot" locations. Preventive patrol could be much more effective if it was similarly concentrated at the places that most needed police attention.

After receiving support from the US National Institute of Justice, Sherman and Weisburd (1995) used crime-mapping technology and statistical analyses to identify 110 crime hot spots for inclusion in the Minneapolis Hot Spots Patrol Experiment. These places were randomly assigned in equal numbers to a control group that would receive normal emergency response service and a treatment group that would receive two to three times that "dosage" of patrol each day. The results of the Minneapolis Hot Spots Patrol Experiment stood in sharp distinction to those of the earlier Kansas City study – Sherman and Weisburd (1995) found a significant relative improvement in the treatment as compared to control hot spots in terms of both crime calls to the police and observations of disorder.

The Minneapolis Hot Spots Patrol Experiment established the importance of crime hot spots for policing. Nevertheless, it was equally important to determine whether directing extra resources to the treated hot spots would simply displace crime problems from one place to another without achieving any overall or lasting reduction in crime. The prevailing criminological view of focused police efforts to control crime was that these actions would inevitably lead to crime displacement. As voiced by Thomas Reppetto (1976: 167), "The police cannot be everywhere ... the foreclosure of one type of criminal opportunity simply shifts the incidence of crime to different forms, times and locales." Ronald V. Clarke and David Weisburd (1994), however, suggested that prospective offenders often overestimate the reach of crime prevention strategies and this misperception led to a "diffusion of crime control benefits" or the reverse of displacement. As such, police resources focused on specific hot spots could result in spillover crime prevention benefits into surrounding areas.

The first hot-spots policing study specifically designed to measure crime displacement and diffusion effects was the Jersey City (New Jersey) Drug Markets Analysis Experiment led by David Weisburd and Lorraine Green (1995).[2] Fifty-six drug hot spots, varying in size from a group of addresses to a group of street segments evidencing high levels of drug activities, were randomly allocated to a treatment group that received a systematic problem-oriented drug market disruption strategy and to a control group that received reactive street-level drug-enforcement tactics. The evaluation showed that the treatment drug hot spots experienced a strong crime prevention benefit relative to the control hot spots. "Displacement catchment areas" of two blocks were constructed around each drug hot spot included in the experiment. Experimental analyses revealed that the treatment catchment areas experienced a significant decrease in both narcotics crime calls and public morals calls in the treatment catchment areas relative to the control catchment areas.

Another study was explicitly designed to shed light on why hot-spots policing does lead to a displacement of crime from target locations. The Jersey City Displacement and Diffusion Project focused on examining the extent to which there was immediate spatial displacement or diffusion as a result of hot-spots policing strategies and why displacement or diffusion occurred or did not occur (Weisburd et al., 2006). Two sites, one with high levels of prostitution and the other with high levels of drug and violent crime, were selected to be targeted and were carefully monitored during an experimental period. Two neighboring areas were selected to serve as catchment areas to assess immediate spatial displacement or diffusion. Intensive police interventions were applied to each target site but not applied to the catchment areas. Over 3,000 twenty-minute social observations were conducted in the target and catchment areas during the study period. These data were supplemented by interviews and ethnographic field observations.

---

[2] Lorraine Green has since changed her name to Lorraine Mazerolle.

The study supported the position that the most likely outcome of such focused crime prevention efforts is a diffusion of crime control benefits to nearby areas. Importantly, the study provided rich qualitative data for understanding why crime does not simply move around the corner in response to focused police interventions implemented at specific crime hot spots. Qualitative data from the Jersey City study suggested that spatial movement from crime sites involves substantial effort and risk by offenders (Weisburd et al., 2006). A number of the offenders that field researchers spoke to complained about the time and effort it would take to reestablish their activities in other areas as a reaction to the police intervention. In essence, offenders were *discouraged* from moving their activities to proximate areas. One respondent arrested at the drug crime site, for example, explained that it is difficult to move because the "money won't be the same," that he "would have to start from scratch," and that it "takes time to build up customers" (Weisburd et al., 2006: 578). Fear of victimization was also an important factor in preventing spatial displacement. One prostitute explained that going to a different area of town was difficult because other prostitutes got angry and told her, "This is our turf, stay away" (Weisburd et al., 2006: 578). Many offenders also suggested that they were *deterred* from committing crime in surrounding areas. In the context of intensive police attention, offenders often assumed that the crackdowns at the hot spots were not limited to the target areas but were part of a more general increase in police activities. As such, they were dissuaded from pursuing crime opportunities in nearby places.

Over the course of the next thirty years, the number of hot-spots policing randomized controlled trials grew exponentially. In 2001, an ongoing systematic review of hot-spots policing studies identified only nine evaluations (five randomized controlled trials and four quasi-experiments; Braga, 2001). By 2019, the number of studies had increased by more than seven times to sixty-five studies (twenty-seven randomized controlled trials and thirty-eight quasi-experiments; Braga et al., 2019). These sixty-five studies included seventy-eight distinct tests of hot-spots policing programs. Some 80 percent of these tests showed significant crime prevention gains generated by the evaluated hot-spots policing programs in treated areas relative to control areas. Crime displacement and diffusion effects were measured in forty-six of the seventy-eight tests (59 percent).

A recent meta-analysis of these tests suggested that hot-spots policing generated a statistically significant 16 percent crime reduction (Braga & Weisburd, 2022) and a Campbell review found a significant diffusion of crime control benefits into surrounding areas (Braga et al., 2019). An independent review of hot-spots policing studies by the National Academies of Sciences, Engineering, and Medicine drew similar conclusions about the crime reduction efficacy of the approach (Weisburd & Majmundar, 2018).

The emerging consensus is that hot-spots policing strategies are effective in controlling crime. However, this knowledge base continues to be strengthened and further developed to get a clearer understanding of the prospects of this approach in creating public safety. Given that these strategies were implemented at a subset of places in larger jurisdictions, it was unclear whether hot-spots policing could result in jurisdiction-wide crime reductions and whether advocates could make plausible claims that the widespread adoption of these programs could be partly responsible for crime reductions in the 1990s and 2000s (Wallman & Blumstein, 2006; Zimring, 2012). Large-scale randomized controlled trials and agent-based simulation models seem to suggest that scaled-up hot-spots policing programs can be used to control jurisdiction-wide crime levels (Ariel et al., 2019b; Weisburd et al., 2017). Though randomized trials are difficult to conduct at this geographic level, they are critical to obtain unbiased estimates of hot-spots policing's wider impact.

### 2.1.2 The Efficacy of Differing Police Strategies to Reduce Crime at Hot Spots

Hot-spots policing research has also tested whether the type of program implemented to prevent crime at places matters in producing crime prevention benefits. The Campbell systematic review noted earlier found that the types of program implemented in the seventy-eight tests of hot-spots policing fell into two broad categories: (1) increased enforcement activities such as heightened levels of patrol, offender apprehension efforts, searches and seizures, and misdemeanor arrests (65 percent) at specific places to prevent crime through general deterrence and increased risk of apprehension; and (2) community problem-solving efforts (35 percent) that attempted to change underlying situations and dynamics causing crime to concentrate at specific places (Braga et al., 2019). Problem-oriented hot-spots policing programs sometimes implement enforcement interventions, and thus can have program components that overlap with the actions taken by increased policing hot-spots programs. Nonetheless, the meta-analysis found that problem-oriented policing generated larger crime prevention impacts at hot spots relative to increased enforcement activities.

The potential for a more powerful impact of policing strategies designed to change places was explored by the Lowell Policing Crime and Disorder Hot Spots Experiment (Braga & Bond, 2008). Thirty-four hot spots were matched into seventeen pairs and one member of each pair was allocated to problem-oriented policing treatment conditions in a randomized block field experiment. The impact evaluation revealed a statistically significant 20 percent reduction in crime and disorder calls for service at the treatment places relative to the control places with no evidence of significant immediate spatial crime displacement. Analyses of systematic observation data also revealed significant reductions in social and physical disorder at the treatment places relative to the control places. The evaluation further suggested that the strongest crime prevention gains at the crime-and-disorder hot spots were driven by situational problem-oriented policing strategies that attempted to modify the criminal opportunity structure in the treatment places by cleaning up vacant lots, improving street lighting, securing abandoned buildings, and making other environmental improvements. Increased misdemeanor arrests had a marginal impact on crime and disorder while police referrals for social service intervention for high-risk people in the places had a null effect.

Other hot-spots policing studies sought to determine whether traditional enforcement strategies could be enhanced to produce stronger crime control impacts at treated places. For instance, a randomized experiment randomly allocating forty-two hot spots to treatment and control conditions in Sacramento, California (Telep et al., 2014) tested the "Koper Curve" suggesting that police officers randomly rotate between hot spots, spending about fifteen minutes patrolling in each (Koper, 1995). Experimental results suggested significant overall declines in both calls for service and crime incidents in the treatment hot spots relative to the controls. A randomized controlled trial in Philadelphia found that offender-focused enforcement in treated hot spots generated significant reductions in violent crime while foot patrol and problem-oriented policing produced null effects in treated hot spots relative to control hot spots (Groff et al., 2015). The evaluators noted that these null effects may have been driven by implementation challenges in the foot patrol and problem-oriented policing conditions. Finally, researchers have explored the potential crime control benefits of "place–network investigations" (PNIs) in crime hot spots that seek to eradicate offender groups' use of crime–place networks that provide the infrastructure necessary to operate illicit markets and promote violent interactions. Promising evidence in Cincinnati and Las Vegas suggests that PNIs may produce significant reductions in violent crime in targeted locations (Herold et al., 2020; Madensen et al., 2017).

### 2.1.3 Current Controversies and Future Directions for Hot-Spots Policing Research

Over the last twenty years, a narrative has been developed that links hot spots policing with unfair, biased, and abusive policing practices (for a discussion, see Weisburd, 2016). Some scholars suggest that hot-spots policing and other intensive police interventions may weaken citizen perceptions of the police

(Kochel, 2011; Rosenbaum, 2019). Enforcement-oriented hot-spots policing programs run the risk of driving a wedge between the police and the communities they serve, with residents of hot-spot areas feeling less like partners and more like targets. This can be particularly problematic in high-crime minority neighborhoods where perceptions of the police are already more negative. What is more, increased enforcement encounters between the police and people of color in crime hot spots may generate concerning racial disparities and unnecessarily expose young black and brown men to the criminal justice system (Briggs & Keimig, 2017). Some pundits have taken the unintended harms observation even further by making unsubstantiated claims that hot-spots policing leads to officers committing "brutal crimes" (see, e.g., Tso, 2016). Other journalists have attempted to draw highly speculative associations between hot-spots policing and the officer-involved deaths of Breonna Taylor in Louisville, Kentucky (Brittain, 2022) and Tyre Nichols in Memphis, Tennessee (Lopez, 2023).

Overly aggressive police enforcement can lead to unintended harmful consequences. For instance, "stop, question, and frisk" (SQF) is a common but controversial proactive policing tactic.[3] Many US police departments began using SQF widely as a proactive policing strategy in the 1990s and early 2000s (Gelman et al., 2007; White & Fradella, 2016). The most influential example of this approach – and how it can go awry – is the NYPD's use of SQF to control crime. Research suggests that the concentration of NYPD stops in crime hot spots was associated with crime reductions (MacDonald et al., 2016; Weisburd et al., 2014b, 2016b). However, the aggressive policing tactics of the NYPD were increasingly criticized as generating large numbers of citizen complaints about police misconduct and abuse of force (Greene, 1999). There were also growing concerns that the NYPD's extensive use of SQF may have been generating unlawful stops that violated Fourth Amendment protections against illegal searches and seizures, and producing racial disparities in who was stopped (Fagan & Davies, 2000; Gelman et al., 2007). A recent systematic review found that SQF programs generated, on average, a significant 13 percent reduction in crime (Weisburd et al., 2023a). This review, however, also found evidence of strong negative health impacts of SQF on individuals and concluded that hot-spots policing initiatives should rely on other kinds of strategy that minimize unintended harms.

---

[3] In the United States, the 1968 *Terry* v. *Ohio* Supreme Court decision allows police officers discretion to conduct an investigatory stop of an individual given reasonable suspicion that the individual has committed a crime or is in the process of committing a crime, and discretion to frisk (or pat down) the individual given reasonable suspicion that they are carrying a weapon.

A growing body of evidence suggests that police legitimacy could be enhanced if officers treated people in ways consistent with procedural justice – that is, providing voice to citizens during encounters, being neutral in decision-making, showing trustworthy motives, and treating people with respect and dignity (Tyler, 2003). A multi-city randomized experiment was designed to determine whether the police could be trained to treat people in fair and respectful ways, and, if so, ascertain whether procedurally just encounters in crime hot spots influenced evaluations of the police and crime (Weisburd et al., 2022). This study randomly allocated 120 crime hot spots to procedural justice and standard conditions in Cambridge, Massachusetts; Houston, Texas; and Tucson, Arizona. The evaluation found that the training led to increased knowledge about procedural justice and more procedurally just behavior in the field as compared with the standard condition. At the same time, procedural justice treatment officers made many fewer arrests than standard policing officers. Residents of the treatment hot spots were significantly less likely to perceive police as harassing or using unnecessary force, but there were no changes in resident perceptions of procedural justice and police legitimacy in the treatment hot spots relative to controls. However, the study did find a significant relative 14 percent decline in crime incidents in the procedural-justice hot spots during the experiment.

A randomized experiment examined whether Assets Coming Together (ACT), a policing intervention directed at increasing collective action and collective efficacy at crime hot spots in Brooklyn Park, Minnesota, would have impacts on police legitimacy, crime, and other outcomes (Weisburd et al., 2021a). While the study did not show increased collective efficacy or perceptions of police legitimacy in the treatment group hot spots, it did find greater participation in crime prevention activities among people who lived in the treatment sites and increases in crime reporting to the police. After adjusting for inflated calls, the evaluation found that police efforts to stimulate collective efficacy produced small but meaningful reductions in crime at the treatment hot spots relative to the control hot spots.

Future hot-spots policing studies need to further consider how the approach can be implemented in ways that maximize crime control gains, minimize harmful enforcement actions, and enhance police legitimacy. Important lessons could be learned in the context of current crime and policing controversies. For instance, gun violence in the United States increased dramatically following the arrival of the COVID-19 pandemic and accelerated after the Black Lives Matter protests over the police murder of George Floyd in 2020. The total number of homicides in the United States surged by almost 30 percent between 2019 and 2020 and then increased by another 7 percent in 2021 (Elinson, 2022). Firearms were used to commit most of these homicides and, by far, black males represented a disproportionate share of the gun homicide victims during this recent wave of violence (Braga & Cook, 2023).

Shootings are highly concentrated in a small number of very stable "hot-spot" locations that generate the bulk of gun violence in cities (e.g., see Braga et al., 2010). Problem-oriented policing can be used to analyze the underlying situations and dynamics that give rise to repeated shootings at violent places and implement tailored strategies to change these conditions (Braga, 2008; Goldstein, 1990). Modifications to physical environments, such as efforts to clean up vacant lots and secure abandoned buildings, can reduce violence at specific places (Braga & Bond, 2008; Braga et al., 2011; Branas et al., 2018). This approach often provides important opportunities to engage communities in strategy development and implementation. It also economizes on the use of costly enforcement actions that could produce unintended harms. Safer public spaces will result in diminished opportunities for guns to be deployed during violent encounters.

Four hot-spots policing studies show that SQF and similar kinds of proactive enforcement activity can be highly effective in reducing gun violence (Cohen & Ludwig, 2002; McGarrell et al., 2001; Rosenfeld et al., 2014; Sherman & Rogan, 1995) and, for the two that considered community perceptions, such efforts were welcomed by residents of persistently violent places (McGarrell et al., 2001; Shaw, 1995). Given the great harms generated by gun violence in affected communities, this raises the question of whether police departments should consider problem-oriented policing supported by lawful stops focused on high-risk people specifically in shooting hot spots (Braga, 2023). Such programs could be used in the short run to generate much needed immediate relief to residents suffering from the ongoing trauma of repeated shootings. It would be critically important for police departments pursuing these activities to focus their actions on high-risk offenders in gun hot spots. This requires additional intelligence gathering and analysis as well as getting to know area residents and people who routinely use these public spaces. Such steps are necessary to avoid indiscriminate and unfocused enforcement efforts that will undermine the legitimacy of the police in the eyes of the citizens who desperately need their help. As problem oriented interventions are implemented and safer public spaces created, police could be more economical in their use of stops to deter people from carrying guns.

Such an approach would require effective police management and community support. Upfront and ongoing training of officers involved in proactive policing efforts would also be required to ensure that encounters in hot-spot locations are conducted lawfully and in a procedurally just manner (Weisburd et al., 2022). Whatever form these new hot-spots policing programs take, it will be critically important for evaluators to use rigorous research designs that include impact and process evaluations that attempt to measure program activities and effects on a wide range of crime, community, and lawfulness outcomes. Before widespread implementation of such approaches, there should be rigorous experimental evaluations that assess crime prevention gains and unintended negative outcomes of policing.

## 2.2 Routinizing Hot-Spots Policing: The Promise of the Pracademic

A focus on micro-places with a sufficient and consistent "dosage" of proactive police initiatives is difficult for police agencies to develop, much less sustain over time (Ariel, 2023b; Greene, 2014). Simply stated, these are often fundamental operational and resourcing considerations (Wain & Ariel, 2014). This section discusses several of these implementation considerations and argues that an essential component for managing these implementation issues is to increase the use of "pracademics," that is, individuals who straddle the boundary between practitioners and academics.[4] In recent years, pracademics have received considerable attention. Pracademics directly apply their academic knowledge to practice (and vice versa) using practical experiences to inform their academic research. In disciplines such as business and medicine, the value of this dual perspective is widely acknowledged, but it is particularly vital for the sector of law enforcement and policing. Pracademics can contribute to the development of comprehensive and cost-effective hot-spots policing strategies by leveraging their interdisciplinary expertise. Pracademics can assist the police by incorporating a surgical approach to territorial policing and capitalizing on the advent of technology to increase efficiencies. In essence, pracademics are vital to ensuring "embeddedness" in hot spots. At a time when the complexities and demands of law enforcement are increasing, pracademics have never been more important. They are invaluable to the applied sciences due to their ability to bridge theory and practice (and translate research into practice) with a nuanced real-world perspective (Piza & Welsh, 2022). Moreover, they offer solutions that can routinize hot-spots policing and overcome the associated costly implementation problems.

To highlight the potential contribution of pracademics in this area, this section focuses on three primary implementation issues in hot-spots policing and the ways in which pracademics can help overcome them. resource, technology/geographic information systems (GIS), and evaluation/monitoring.

---

[4] Section 2.2 was drafted by Barak Ariel.

First, however, the section focuses on the role of the pracademic in evidence-based practice generally and in hot-spots policing specifically.

### 2.2.1 Pracademics and Their Role in Evidence-Based Practice

The pracademic can be described as wearing two hats simultaneously: that of a skilled practitioner in an applied practice and that of a productive researcher with training in theory and research methods (Boursnell & Birch, 2020; Posner, 2009). This polycephaly (i.e., having two heads) can be found in virtually all disciplines where applied research is relevant: physicians who are also professors of medicine, engineers who conduct primary research on applied materials, psychotherapists who see patients and supervise students as part of their training, and police officers who also contribute to the production of science. Indeed, there is more than one type of pracademic. They can be academics embedded in field settings, but they can also be practitioners who contribute to science.

Pracademics are found between two extremes of a continuum. On one side of the spectrum are "pure" academics, who have attained a high level of expertise in their discipline. They typically possess advanced degrees, such as a PhD, and are engaged in scholarly activities, including theorizing, teaching, and contributing to the knowledge and discourse of their field through advancing theory and philosophy (Dickinson et al., 2022; Levander, 2022).

On the other side of the spectrum are "pure" professionals, who have specialized practical knowledge or expertise in a specific field or occupation. They typically exhibit a high level of competence and skill, and adhere to the profession's established standards, ethics, and practices. However, they lack academic credentials, which means that they are likely to exhibit developed expertise and competence in a specific occupation through practical experience, on-the-job training, or self-study rather than through formal academic education. They acquire this substantial practical experience by working in their field over a significant period of time, which allows them to develop a deep understanding of their profession and the skills required to perform their work effectively. However, despite not having formal academic credentials, pure professionals actively engage in ongoing professional development. They may attend workshops, seminars, industry conferences, and relevant training programs to enhance their knowledge and skills. They may have undergone an apprenticeship or worked closely with experienced professionals who have shared their knowledge, skills, and insights. These types of mentorship help shape their understanding and mastery of the relevant profession.

Between these extremes, there are many kinds of pracademic, blending elements of academia and professional practice to varying degrees. The specific roles within each category may vary depending on the field, industry, and individual circumstances, and the categories represent varying degrees of integration between academia and professional practice. For example, there may be academics who actively engage with professionals and industry experts, collaborate/consult on research projects, and contribute their expertise to areas beyond academia. These types of academic maintain connections with practitioners and apply their research to real-world contexts. There are also professionals who actively engage with academic institutions by participating in research collaborations and contributing to peer-reviewed publications or by taking on adjunct teaching positions. Finally, a category in the middle of the continuum is the hybrid academic–professional. These types hold positions that blur the line between academia and professional practice. They could include academics who split their time between teaching and consulting, researchers embedded within industry settings, and professionals who conduct research in academic settings while maintaining active professional roles.

### 2.2.1.1 The Strategic Role of Pracademics in Policing

Pracademics are indispensable to evidence-based policing. Their dual expertise can contribute substantially to the development of policies, operational strategies, and training programs. Academics in law enforcement frequently have direct knowledge of the complexities and difficulties of policing. Alongside academic expertise, their direct knowledge of on-the-ground realities enables them to devise informed, practical, and effective strategies (Willis, 2016).

In law enforcement, the main pracademic type is the professional with academic engagement, such as a uniformed police officer who has training in theory and research methods in scholastic circles (Piza et al., 2021). These practitioners contribute to the academic sphere by conducting research ingrained in the realities of practice, with a finer understanding of the realpolitik of law enforcement (Drover & Ariel, 2015). They provide practical perspectives that are lacking in academic research, leading to insights that full-time academics may have overlooked (Jackson, 2010). They can assist academics in comprehending the practical challenges and limitations of policing, resulting in more relevant and applicable research (Magnusson, 2020). However, given their footing in academia, pracademics use the most recent theories, research findings, and evidence-based practices to enhance their work in the professional realm (Huey & Mitchell, 2016). They serve as conduits, translating academic knowledge into a form that is readily comprehended and applicable by practitioners (Braga, 2016).

### 2.2.1.2 The Benefits of Pracademics in Hot-Spots Policing

As the pracademic becomes familiarized with the robust science behind hot spots in general (Weisburd, 2015) and hot-spots policing in particular (Braga et al., 2019; Sherman & Weisburd, 1995), they can exploit their position within their professional institution to advance, promote, and potentially lead the necessary changes toward institutionalizing hot-spot practices (Bond & Nader, 2018; Byrne & Marx, 2011; Famega et al., 2017). This intersection provides a unique position where they can apply academic knowledge directly to real-world situations that characterize hot-spots policing and use their professional experience to influence academic inquiry into the broader issues of this tactic.

Hot-spots policing, by its very nature, emphasizes the use of empirical research and scientific methodologies. To identify hot spots (in the contemporary GIS sense, rather than the archaic "pins on maps" approach of the 1980s), advanced skills in spatial analysis are required (Ariel et al., 2016; Harinam et al., 2022; Macbeth & Ariel, 2019; Weinborn et al., 2017). In this context, pracademics are ideally suited to implement these analytical capabilities due to their dual perspectives; for example, they can inform computer-generated maps about practical obstacles in reaching the hot spot or about the jurisdictional composition of the area that may alter patrol strategies; they can also provide insights into recent intelligence patterns that may hinder the ability of officers to affect crime at the hot spots (Bland et al., 2022). With their knowledge of research methodologies, they can help identify underlying issues, evaluate the efficacy of current strategies, and propose solutions supported by evidence. In turn, this can result in more-efficient and more-effective strategies (Kuchar, 2020).

Additionally, pracademics can cultivate a learning culture within law-enforcement agencies. They can advocate for the importance of research and evidence-based practices among colleagues and provide training/support for those who are unfamiliar with these concepts. Collectively, they can act as the "Paul Reveres" of evidence-based policing. In other words, they spread the call for more evidence-based interventions in policing and ensure that they are implemented, which, in turn, can help improve the overall competence and professionalism of the police force (Lam, 2021).

### 2.2.2 The Pracademic as a Vehicle to Respond to Primary Implementation Issues in Hot-Spots Policing

We now return to implementation issues within hot-spots policing. We will also examine how pracademics can provide solutions to the obstacles presented.

### 2.2.2.1 The Implementation Issues: Costs

In an age of resource austerity typified by competing demands and a shrinking force size in many police departments, hot-spots policing and proactive policing more broadly are "the first to go" in freeing up capabilities for response duties (Ariel, 2023b). The fact that prevention is more cost-effective than dealing with crime after the fact is an insufficient condition for investing in an expensive program such as hot-spots policing. Consider, for instance, budgetary considerations, where the implementation of hot-spots policing necessitates increased financial resources. In this context, organizations must allocate funds for personnel salaries (often costed as overtime expenditure, number of officers allocated, or number of dedicated resources), training programs, technology investments, community initiatives, and ongoing evaluation efforts – not to mention opportunity costs. The resource implications of instituting hot-spots policing can vary based on context, the scope of implementation, and the law-enforcement agency's available resources, but, overall, it is essential to carefully plan and allocate resources to guarantee effective and sustainable implementation.

Furthermore, hot-spots policing typically requires a dedicated team of law-enforcement officers or a requirement from available officers to dedicate their time to attending the hot spots. However, perhaps unlike some US police departments (e.g., Weisburd et al., 2015b), UK police forces, for example, are struggling to identify unallocated time for constables to attend to hot spots. To effectively cover the specified hot spots, it may be necessary to reassign existing personnel or hire additional officers, which, in many contemporary police agencies, would be a struggle.

### 2.2.2.2 The Implementation Issues: Technology and GIS

To identify and monitor crime hot spots, relatively advanced technology and data-analysis tools are frequently required. It may be necessary for agencies to invest in software, hardware, and data infrastructure to effectively collect, analyze, and visualize crime data. Establishing and maintaining communication channels and exchanging pertinent data may also require additional information technology (IT) resources. Examples include obtaining data from partner agencies such as health professions (Ariel et al., 2015; Boyle et al., 2013), private security agencies (Ariel et al., 2017), or third-party treatment providers (Ariel, 2023b). Thus, for successful hot-spots policing, information sharing between law-enforcement agencies and other relevant stakeholders, such as community organizations and social services, may be required and, in this respect, allocating resources to capture data is a timely and expensive exercise (Strang et al., 2017).

### 2.2.2.3 The Implementation Issue: Evaluation and Monitoring

It is essential to evaluate the cost-effectiveness and efficacy of hot-spots policing initiatives on an ongoing basis. Many UK police forces, for example, have insights and analysis teams that assist frontline officers in analytical capabilities (Piza & Feng, 2017). Allocating resources for these activities, especially in regard to the impact of these interventions – for example crime variations, community satisfaction, and officer performance – can provide invaluable insights for refining strategies and efficiently allocating resources. However, these come with a substantial opportunity cost: if a dedicated analyst is seconded to the hot-pot-policing project then they are not free to conduct analyses for other purposes.

### 2.2.3 Pracademics and Their Roles in Resolving Implementation Issues

By combining their practical experience and academic knowledge, a pracademic can provide valuable insights, research-based recommendations, and evidence-driven approaches to address the key considerations involved in implementing hot-spots policing (den Heyer 2022). Therefore, all types of pracademic can be seen as essential components for the systematization of hot-spots policing as a routine practice in policing. Where there are pracademics, hot-spots policing is more likely to flourish, and the barriers to implementation are more likely to be removed. Cambridge University "Pracademia" is a case in point (Ariel et al., 2019a); it was a program that successfully trained and embedded pracademics in multiple police departments where hot-spots policing was routinized (Sherman, 2021).

### 2.2.3.1 Resources

Project management – perhaps the most overlooked yet crucial role of the pracademic – relates to the pracademic's ability to combine practical experience with the rigor of an academic project to lead and manage hot-spots policing effectively. By integrating research, data analysis, collaboration, and evaluation, they can manage the evidence-based strategies that contribute to crime reduction and community safety at the micro-spatial level while maintaining the authoritarian paradigm that characterizes policing, where constables are tasked with attending to hot spots. According to Brants and Ariel (2023), this is referred to as "building bridges" in the context of embedded intermediaries.

Effective project management necessitates robust collaboration with multiple stakeholders. The pracademic project manager facilitates communication and coordination between law-enforcement agencies, community partners, researchers, and other pertinent parties. They cultivate partnerships to ensure that the initiative is successful and provide a forum for the exchange of knowledge and best practices. This collaborative approach ensures that knowledge and resources are shared effectively, leading to sustainable and cost-effective hot-spots policing initiatives.

### 2.2.3.2 Reduce Budgetary Constraints

A pracademic project manager can analyze resource requirements and allocate them efficiently. By conducting a thorough needs assessment based on past hot-spot experiments, and by understanding the expected outcomes of the project before it is rolled out, they can streamline resource allocation, ensuring that resources such as personnel, equipment, and technology are utilized effectively. This approach minimizes wastage and unnecessary expenditures. Furthermore, they can leverage internal expertise, instead of relying heavily on external consultancy companies. The pracademic project manager can tap into the expertise available within the police department, and, by capitalizing on the knowledge and skills of experienced officers and staff, they can reduce the need for costly external consultants. This approach not only saves money but also fosters professional development and strengthens internal capabilities.

Similarly, the pracademic project manager can establish partnerships with academic institutions. This collaboration can provide access to academic experts and researchers who can contribute their knowledge and skills without the need for expensive consultancy services. Academic institutions often have resources and expertise that can be utilized in project implementation, such as data analysis, evaluation frameworks, and research support, where the "payment" for their services is the ability to publish the results in peer-reviewed journals. These "low-cost experiments" (Ariel, 2011) may be unpopular among university provosts, but they provide a potentially potent framework for producing evidence in otherwise poorly funded research environments.

Above all, a person with a footing inside the organization can streamline processes. The pracademic is essential for minimizing costs and maximizing efficiency. They can facilitate clear communication channels, well-defined roles and responsibilities, and efficient decision-making mechanisms. This ensures that tasks are executed promptly, thereby minimizing delays and reducing opportunity costs associated with project management.

### 2.2.3.3 Technology and GIS

Technology can significantly reduce costs in hot-spots policing initiatives. The pracademic project manager can identify and leverage cost-effective technology solutions for data analysis, information-sharing, and communication. By adopting efficient software tools, data-management systems, and communication platforms, they can optimize operational efficiency and reduce the costs associated with traditional manual processes. A pracademic can thus evaluate different technology solutions and data-analysis methods to identify cost-effective options. Due to this assessment, agencies can invest in technologies that enhance hot-spots policing operations while optimizing resource allocation. Indeed, they can leverage their academic knowledge and expertise to assess and recommend appropriate technology and data-analysis tools for hot-spots policing.

### 2.2.3.4 Evaluation and Assessment

Possibly the most straightforward way that pracademics can contribute to cost reduction is through their skills in measurement and evaluations. Via interdisciplinary expertise, a pracademic can contribute to the development of comprehensive and cost-effective hot-spots policing strategies. This is because they can conduct research on the effectiveness of different intervention approaches, such as problem-oriented policing, community policing, and targeted enforcement, to identify the most efficient methods for crime prevention (Magnusson, 2020).

Pracademics can analyze crime data and identify emerging hot spots. By utilizing their analytical skills and knowledge of advanced data-analysis techniques, they can help agencies identify areas at risk of becoming hot spots and allocate resources accordingly. This proactive approach can prevent crime from escalating and minimize the need for costly reactive responses. For example, a pracademic can assist in developing performance metrics and evaluation frameworks to assess the impact of hot-spots policing initiatives (Norton et al., 2018). By measuring outputs and outcomes, they can provide empirical evidence of the cost-effectiveness of these strategies. This information can guide resource-allocation decisions and demonstrate the value of investing in hot-spots policing.

Pracademics can also contribute to the evaluation and monitoring of hot-spots policing initiatives by conducting rigorous research and analysis. In particular, they can develop evaluation frameworks, design surveys/data collection methods, and analyze the collected data to assess the effectiveness of hot-spots policing strategies. Their academic expertise can ensure that evaluation efforts are conducted objectively and provide meaningful insights for future resource allocation. Lastly, pracademics can actively participate in policy discussions and provide evidence-based recommendations for resource allocation in hot-spots policing. Their expertise can inform decision-makers about the cost-effectiveness of this prevention strategy, ensuring that limited resources are allocated where they will have the greatest impact (Douglas & Braga, 2021).

### 2.2.4 Some Limitations Regarding the Involvement of Pracademics in Hot-Spots Policing

Integrating pracademics in police agencies is not an instant remedy to the challenges we have noted, and it can be costly. To encourage the integration of pracademics, police agencies must invest in continuing education and support for development of knowledge and integration into academic networks of communication such as conferences and training seminars (Ansell & Gash, 2018). Creating and then utilizing pracademics is a strategic transition; with a constant influx of pracademics into policing, the development of evidence-based practices can potentially be enhanced. Still, the temporal delay between training and implementation does not provide a practical way to address immediate concerns.

In turn, pushback from peers, coworkers, and superiors often derives from the conventional policing culture, which is likely to favor experience over evidence-based tactics (Ariel, 2023a). Police culture often exhibits resistance to the changes proposed by pracademics, who argue for a more analytical approach to crime prevention and law enforcement (Willis, 2016). Similarly, police chiefs encounter constraints in their ability to enact modifications due to employment restrictions, budgetary determinations made by elected authorities, and the power dynamics inherent in police forces. The limitations imposed by these restraints can hinder the efforts of pracademics to develop police innovations including hot-spots policing, by restricting their capacity to control and implement policy changes inside their departments. The inherent hierarchical structure of police organizations is such that, even with the push of pracademics to do "the right thing," decisions frequently undergo a series of approvals, which can impede innovation and cause delays in implementing programs advanced by pracademics.

### 2.2.5 Conclusions

The significance of pracademics in policing and law enforcement cannot be overstated. By combining academic knowledge with practical experience, they can overcome implementation challenges to hot-spots policing. Pracademics are uniquely positioned to reconcile the significant divide between theory and practice. They can translate academic research into applicable strategies/solutions, and can utilize their firsthand experiences to inform and enrich their academic work. They can also contribute to a more nuanced understanding of law-enforcement challenges and suggest effective approaches to addressing them. Pracademics are critical for the successful development and implementation of hot-spots policing.

## 3 Crime, Place, and Prevention Outside Policing

## 3.1 Place, Power, Crime, and Control: The Importance of Proprietary Places

There are many types of place. Some are large, like neighborhoods. Some are small, like street segments. Some are tiny, like addresses. These are *pooled*, *proximal*, and *proprietary* places, respectively (Madensen & Eck, 2013). This section is about proprietary places.[5] If pooled places are macro, and proximal places are micro, then proprietary places are *nano*-places. They are the smallest type of place for which we can measure crime reliably.

Charles Booth, studying late-nineteenth-century London, was the first to link proprietary places to crime (LSE Library, 2016). Then W. E. B. DuBois applied Booth's methods to a largely African American ward in Philadelphia (Du Bois, 1973 [1899]). Both researchers found criminogenic addresses in and among crime uninvolved addresses. If researchers had followed up on these leads we would know more about crime today.

A hundred years elapsed before two teams of researchers rediscovered the importance of proprietary places. Sherman and colleagues (1989), using Minneapolis data, demonstrated that, regardless of crime type, most addresses and intersections have no crime but a few addresses and intersections have a great deal of crime. About the same time, Glenn Pierce and colleagues (1988) showed that this was true in Boston. Numerous other studies have confirmed this concentration at the level of specific addresses (Eck et al., 2007; Lee et al., 2017). Wilcox and Eck (2011) have described this concentration of crime at addresses as following a "law of troublesome places," and this phenomenon can be seen more generally as part of a "law of crime concentration at places" (Weisburd, 2015; see also Weisburd et al., 2012).

This section begins by reviewing what we have learned about proprietary places since 1990. To reduce word clutter, the section drops the adjective *proprietary*, adding it only when the reader needs to be reminded of this distinction. Following the review, eight questions for future research on nano-places are discussed (Sections 3.1.2.1–3.1.2.8). In the conclusions (Section 3.1.3) it is suggested that examining proprietary places has vital implications for our understanding of social control.

### 3.1.1 Proprietary Places and Crime

A proprietary place has three essential characteristics. First, it has an owner: a person, family, corporation, government, or nongovernment organization. This

---

[5] Section 3.1 was drafted by John Eck.

may be its most essential characteristic, as ownership establishes who has power to control the physical and social environment. Second, it has a limited number of functions. These functions are established by the place owners and operators: the place managers. Homes are for families to live in. Stores are for selling things. Bars and pubs are places to drink. Hospitals are for treating the sick. When a proprietary place has more than one function, one function is more critical than the others; if that function fails, all the others fail. A church, for example, may have services on Sundays, serve as a daycare center on weekdays, and host meetings for people fighting drug and alcohol dependence on Wednesday evenings. If this place ceases to be a church, in all likelihood the other functions will cease. Third, a place has a perimeter, inside of which the owner has authority, and outside of which they do not. As a consequence of these three characteristics, most proprietary places are small. Many will fit on a street segment and hundreds fit within a neighborhood (Eck et al., 2023).

Why is crime concentrated at a small proportion of proprietary places, leaving most places crime-free? The explanation for this concentration is the way in which proprietary places are managed (Eck et al., 2023). Place managers are people who own or operate proprietary places. Ownership confers on place managers the authority to control the behaviors within the place.

Ownership consists of a bundle of rights (Demsetz, 1967; Honoré, 1961; Waldron, 1988). An owner can transfer these rights – permanently through sale, or temporarily through leasing, renting, contracting, or employing. A store clerk has place management authority because they have an employment agreement with the store owner. The store owner either owns the property or leases it from the building's owner.

Place management theory asserts that property rights, and the authority these rights convey, are central to social control. This makes proprietary places *loci of control*, as David Weisburd described my theory about ten years ago. Rather than control arising from the state's enforcement of criminal law, or from residents' socializing, place management theory asserts that much control – perhaps most – comes from the actions of people and institutions who own and control property. Property rights are enforceable by courts, so place management authority depends on how the state regulates private property. But it is neither formal control nor informal control, as criminologists use these terms (Eck et al., 2023).

This idea has its roots in the work of Jane Jacobs (1956) who forcefully pointed out that it was shopkeepers who keep the peace on the street. Five years later, she expanded this idea in her famous book *Death and Life of Great American Cities* (Jacobs, 1961). Though misinterpreted by generations of criminologists, Jacobs gave numerous examples of shopkeepers – not pedestrians or residents – being the eyes on the street (Linning & Eck, 2021). She asserted that urban renewal and public housing were destroying shops, removing shopkeepers, and creating unsafe streets.

Place management is not another form of guardianship. Managers do not need to be present at their places to thwart crime at their places. Although place managers may act as guardians (Jacobs, 1961), hire guardians, or train their staff to be guardians, guardianship is not their sole means of control. Place managers exercise control by deciding how to configure their physical spaces, how to regulate place users' behaviors within their place, who to admit or bar from their place, and how they will acquire resources to operate their place (Madensen & Eck, 2013). Guardianship is but one of many tools place managers use to thwart crime. Importantly, and conversely, a guardian cannot create place management without acquiring property rights. Therefore, it is best to consider guardianship and place management as distinct mechanisms, even if they do overlap.

We know that place managers can influence crime. We have a large number of studies, most of which are quasi-experimental or randomized experiments, that show that when place managers alter critical features of their places, crime goes down (Douglas & Welsh, 2022; Eck, 2002; Eck & Guerette, 2012).

That place managers are important for curbing crime should not come as a surprise. You see their influence every day. Stores are arranged to guide your movement. Store shelves are stocked to tempt you. Curb cuts are placed to allow you easy entry and exit from parking. Signs direct you where to go and what to do. Clerks, bartenders, wait staff, airline attendants, landlords, and a cavalcade of other place managers offer you assistance and divert you from misbehavior. Much of your everyday life is structured by place managers.

Nor should it be a surprise that place managers keep order. Much of what we know about place management has its origins in police efforts to solve difficult crime and disorder problems (Eck, 2015). What may be surprising, though, given these origins, is that the future of proprietary place research opens up a series of crime prevention approaches that are not directly connected to policing.

### 3.1.2 Questions In Need of Answers

Where do we go next? The development and testing of place management theory reveals eight lines of future research.

#### 3.1.2.1 How Do Place Managers Make Crime Prevention Choices?

We have a theory of place management that describes its functions (Madensen & Eck, 2008). We have experiments that show that place management influences crime (Douglas & Welsh, 2022). But what are good place managers doing every day that is different from what bad place managers do?

A few qualitative and mixed methods studies try to answer these questions. For example, Jacques and Moeller (2023) examine coffee shops in Amsterdam, and Ceccato and colleagues (2023) look into libraries. But we need more researchers peering into the black box and observing the mundane mechanisms of management. We need investigations to determine how place managers anticipate crime, adjust to crime, or promote crime. We need to know how crime prevention fits into their business strategy, their incentives and disincentives for curbing crime. Knowing these things will help us craft useful policies.

### 3.1.2.2 Who Owns Crime?

How concentrated is crime among place owners? While most property owners possess a single place, there are many people and organizations who own multiple properties. Economists have known for a very long time that, regardless of the business, a few dominate their markets (Simon & Bonini, 1958). Those who study urban spaces also know that, in any metropolitan area, a small fraction of property owners possesses most of the property (Gilderbloom, 1989). Indeed, Pareto (1909) observed more than a hundred years ago that 80 percent of the property in Italy was controlled by 20 percent of the owners. This is important because if crime is concentrated at the level of property owner, then owner-level interventions become key policy options.

We have a few studies on this topic. Payne and Eck (2007) reported that, in Cincinnati, 10 percent of the rental property owners had 100 percent of the violent and 46 percent of the property crime. Payne and his colleagues (2013) also reported that, in a small town near Cincinnati, calls to police were concentrated among a small fraction of property owners. A team of researchers from Northeastern University (Zoorob & O'Brien, 2023) have demonstrated that, in Boston, crime is concentrated among owners. Lee et al. (2022) showed that this sort of concentration was common regardless of the property type examined.

Of the questions listed, this may be the easiest one to answer. The procedure is to aggregate crime to the level of address, and then aggregate addresses to the level of owner. As long as crime, place, and owner data are available, and there are identifiers that can link the datasets, this is not a difficult process. The major difficulty is that many of the owners may be legal corporations (limited liability corporations [LLCs]), and LLCs can own other LLCs. Connecting owners to higher-level owners is a tedious and difficult task that needs to be undertaken. So is the examination of crime concentration among owners across regions and countries.

### 3.1.2.3 Are Some Crime-Involved Places Invisible?

Since the late 1980s, researchers interested in proprietary place research have used police data: reports of crimes or calls by the public to request police assistance. However, there are crime-involved places that do not generate large numbers of calls to the police. In 2013, Eck and Madensen classified crime-involved places. *Crime sites* are the high-crime places with many calls. *Convergence settings*, first identified by Marcus Felson (2003), are public locations where people routinely meet and offenders can too (Bichler et al., 2014). A central public transportation hub is an example. And so are some nightclubs. These places may report some crime, but they may not. *Comfort spaces*, suggested by Matt Hammer (2011), are private hangouts of offenders. They are used to stash illegal goods, to relax, or as surveillance posts to view potential targets or police activity. Finally, *corrupting spots* are private places for transacting illegal business: for example, a metal recycling yard serving as a market for stolen goods.

The importance of these hidden crime-involved places is obvious. They can simulate crime at other places. Nevertheless, they are invisible to an analyst using police call data. So research into these places is thin. But crime suppression efforts need to take such places into account.

Researchers have two choices. They can ferret out hidden crime places using qualitative and mixed methods studies. This will require talking to community members, including offenders, as well as observing small areas. Or they can rely on police intelligence information.

### 3.1.2.4 Do Crime-Involved Places Form Networks?

We study places in isolation. But if crime-involved places have different functions, then crime-involved places may be connected. This was the insight of Tamara and Maris Herold, when Maris was a police district commander in Cincinnati. She and Tamara speculated that a persistently violent hot spot may resist police efforts because it involves multiple places, each serving different functions. This led to their creation of place–network investigations (PNIs) in Cincinnati. Their team, made up of police and other city officials and supported by a governing board that included community members, investigated the places in extremely violent spots (often including one or two square blocks). By addressing the place infrastructure of crime, the PNI project scored some notable successes. The successes were notable because they were sustained for more months than is typical and because the project did not focus on arresting people (Hammer, 2020). The PNI team won the Herman Goldstein Award for Problem Solving Excellence in 2017 (Hammer et al., 2017), and is now being trialed in other cities.

If PNIs prove to be a reliably effective strategy for suppressing violence, the importance of place networks will be obvious. Researchers can await the outcomes of evaluations or they can study such networks. This too will require either qualitative work in the field or partnering with investigative agencies.

### 3.1.2.5 Do High-Crime Places Radiate Crime into Neighborhoods?

There is a very large body of research asking questions like does the presence of a particular land use increase crime in neighborhoods (Eck et al., 2023, 2024; Linning et al., 2024)? The earliest studies were of drinking places (Roncek, 1981). A recent study examined churches (Wo, 2023). Bars and churches, it turns out, are criminogenic. The question we are asking here is different. We are asking if high-crime-involved places promote trouble outside the place. Does a high-crime bar (or church) create more crime in its surroundings than a no-crime bar (or church)?

Although this question seems obvious, there is only a single study directly answering it. Bowers (2014) asked whether high-theft places create more thefts nearby. In a large British city, she found that they did. Although the volume of crime at the high-crime places mattered, what mattered more was the number of high-crime places in the area.

Policymakers wanting to reduce crime in areas could use research like Bowers' to create useful strategies. But, as Bowers (2014) shows, it is difficult to tease out the causal ordering – making sure it is the places causing the area crime and not the other way around. This requires large datasets and several years of crime data at places.

### 3.1.2.6 Can We Regulate Crime Places?

There is considerable evidence that policing hot spots of crime does help reduce crime (Braga & Weisburd, 2022; Braga et al., 2019). However, just because it is evidence-based does not mean that we should be using this tactic as a primary method of crime control. It may be superior to patrolling entire neighborhoods, but we need even better strategies.

If hot spots are created by hot dots within them (Lee & Eck, 2019), then patrolling spots may be less effective than removing the dots. Regulating the managers of the dots maybe a useful strategy. Over a decade ago, Eck and Eck (2012) showed how environmental regulatory policies could be adapted to crime reduction and that all but one of these policies have been used to thwart crime.

Shifting to a regulatory approach may increase effectiveness and may reduce the need to impose criminal justice sanctions. Given the increasing skepticism about the role of the police, and legitimate demands for feasible alternatives to policing, we need a great deal of experimentation and innovation in the regulatory area.

### 3.1.2.7 Can Safe Places Radiate Safety?

All the questions so far dwell on the negative: crime-involved places. Do the many crime-free places have no impact? A thought experiment clarifies this question. Imagine a very-high-crime neighborhood in which a few high-crime places, with supporting crime-involved places, generate crime throughout the area. Removing these bad places would reduce crime considerably. But if the places were not recycled for good purposes – if they just stood vacant – what would be the result? Linning and Eck (2021) suggest that these places need to be put to good use because well-run places can exude safety. They radiate safety in four ways (see also Eck et al., 2023). First, the owner of the place has an interest in the safety of their immediate surroundings. Jane Jacobs (1961) underscored this point. Second, the owner can purchase other nearby places, expanding safety to them by applying sound management practices. Third, the owner may join a network of place managers who work together to promote safety in their area. And last, owners are connected to financial institutions and government agencies that have an interest in area safety.

Crime researchers have made little headway in the study of residents' production of order (Linning et al., 2022). We have many multivariate studies, but no actionable results. If place management can spread order, we have a potential policy. Criminologists seldom investigate how property owners operate, acquire property, create networks, or fit into the larger political economy (Linning & Eck, 2023). This question suggests that they should.

### 3.1.2.8 Can Place Management Theory Be Applied to Cybercrime?

In addressing this point, we have assumed that we are dealing with a physical place. But what about the cyber world? Eck and Clarke (2003) note that routine activity theory was largely about crime within an arm's length: the offender had to be physically close to their target to strike it, take (from) it, or deface it. But what about crimes that occur at a distance, such as mail bombings and Internet crimes? Eck and Clarke (2003) show that if you substitute "network" for "place" in the theory then the theory still applies: the offender and the target encounter each other on the same network in the absence of effective controllers. The owner of the network has the same core functions as the owner of a physical place. So, in principle, much of what we know about place management in the physical world can be tweaked to fit the cyber world (Eck & Clarke,

2003). Recently, researchers have begun to apply place management theory to cyber worlds (Bichler, 2021; Ho et al., 2023; Reyns, 2010; Reyns et al., 2011).

Criminologists are used to downloading police data to study places. To study place management in cyber worlds, they will have to find ways to explore privately held data. Most of the progress in answering this question will come from researchers within private organizations or academics who are providing valuable consulting services to these organizations.

### 3.1.3 Social Control

Place management is a form of control that does not fit into criminology's distinction between state (formal) and residents' (informal) control (Eck et al., 2023). It is a third control mechanism. Although it does not invalidate formal or informal control, it challenges them. It discomforts formal control by suggesting that some of the control we expect from policing may originate from owners of property. After all, property owners make good use of the police. It questions how much influence residents have over crime in high-crime areas. Where most residents do not control property (Desmond, 2017), they depend on landlords and other business owners for control. Residents are not powerless, however. Their power comes from political mobilization to change how the state and the place managers behave (see Hunter, 2013).

## 3.2 The Role of Local Government Investment in Crime Prevention

In recent years there has been renewed interest in reimagining public safety.[6] Most of the attention has been focused on altering funding for police agencies. However, local governments also play a pivotal role via the fairness and equity with which they provide services and regulate the quality of the built environment. Indeed, these powers have been successfully harnessed to reduce crime in hot spots. Logically, then, an examination of whether the provision of local government services might prevent the formation of crime hot spots seems a prudent avenue of investigation.

Both theory and extant research have established a relationship between specific characteristics of the built environment and crime concentrations. Seminal work by Jane Jacobs (1961) highlighted the connection between features of the built environment and crime. Taylor and Gottfredson (1986) elaborated how the characteristics of street blocks and specific locations within

---

[6] Section 3.2 was drafted by Elizabeth Groff. Opinions contained in this section are those of the author and do not necessarily reflect those of the National Institute of Justice or the Department of Justice.

the street block affected the perceived crime opportunity at places. MacDonald (2015) summarized evidence produced by quasi-experiments that demonstrate how changes to the built environment can reduce crime.

The routine efforts of state and local government can help to prevent crime. Sampson (1990) noted the importance of these "crime effects of non-crime policies." The work of local government agencies can be divided into two broad types. First is provision of public amenities such as street repair, garbage collection, street lights, libraries, and parks and recreation. Second is regulation of the quality of the built environment via controls on residents, property owners, and business owners. These activities affect the quality of the built environment either directly or indirectly.

Over the last fifty years there have been various styles of policing that attempt to actively involve other city agencies in solving public-safety issues. Neighborhood team policing (Bloch & Specht, 1973; Sherman et al., 1973), third-party policing (Buerger & Mazerolle, 1998), and PNIs (Herold et al., 2020) all emphasize interaction with city agencies to solve specific community problems at specific places. These targeted efforts have been successful at reducing crime.

The success of involving local government agencies in crime reduction efforts suggests that the *routine* provision of government services may be effective in preventing the emergence of crime hot spots. However, there has been almost no research conducted that examines the routine distribution of municipal services to the urban place and its relationship to crime. Such examinations are at the heart of a move to a more holistic discussion of community safety that extends beyond police departments, to local governments more generally.

### 3.2.1 Role of Government Services in Everyday Life

Local governments are critical to public health and safety because they have authority over and responsibility for the built environment. One way this authority is expressed is through regulations. Governments can regulate the quality of structures, the disorder levels, the types of business, and the geographic distribution of land uses. The earliest regulations were fire-related, but their scope expanded during the Progressive Era (Glaeser, 2013). The first city-wide zoning plan was implemented by New York City in 1916. Zoning restricts the types of land use and the density of land use allowed for each parcel. It also specifies building setbacks and other structure-specific regulations. Local governments can regulate new and existing businesses via licensing requirements.

Criminology

This tool is typically applied to alcohol-serving establishments but can also affect business types with the potential to affect public health and safety.

Local governments provide a wide array of services that affect the quality of life experienced by everyone who lives or works in a city. City services create and maintain the infrastructure on which users depend. Examples of infrastructure elements include streets, bridges, bike lanes, bike trails, street lighting, curbs and gutters, stormwater systems, water and sewer systems, fire hydrants, trash cans, and sidewalks. In addition, local governments provide amenities that enhance the quality of life such as cemeteries, libraries, parks, recreation centers, and schools. Other city services provide public transportation (buses), dispose of refuse (garbage collection, street cleaning), prevent and mitigate the damage from fires (fire departments), and maintain order (police). Finally, some services involve the enforcement of regulations that require private owners to maintain their property such as housing, fire, nuisance, and other types of code inspector to maintain the overall health and safety of the city.

After the civil rights movement in the 1960s, political scientists began examining the distribution of municipal services across the city. Such distributional questions are important for several reasons. First, quantifying them allows us to examine "who gets what, when, how" (Lasswell, 1936) as well as "where" (Smith, 1974). Second, "municipal services are collectively a key determinant of the quality of urban life" (Lineberry & Welch, 1974: 701). Third, the distribution of government effort is a symbolic representation of the relative attention individuals and places are receiving (Jones, 1977). Differentials in government effort are noticed and contribute to the ecological labels that develop and affect private investment. Finally, the presence of systemic racism and structural disadvantage suggests that an empirical examination of the distribution of services is prudent.

City services have a very large impact on the quality of life experienced by residents. To the extent that those services are not equitably distributed, some residents have a better quality of life than others, which is fundamentally unfair (Lineberry & Welch, 1974). Some distributional effects are due to racial and income homogeneity within neighborhoods (Jones, 1977). For example, adding a library will improve community-wide access to libraries, but the impact of that library will be greatest on the people who live near the new library branch, resulting in distributional impacts.

The Kerner Commission (1968) found that inequities in the distribution of services contributed to poverty by depriving some residents of some parts of the city of services that other residents get. This also means that those who are not getting have to go without or pay for those services on the private market. Poor residents who cannot afford to buy services to level the playing field are doubly disadvantaged.

### 3.2.2 Quantifying Service Distribution

Previous research has focused on the "whether" and the "why" of service provision (Lineberry, 1977: 49). Whether city services are differentially allocated is the first question. The second concerns why that is the case. A third, more recent question focuses on where services are over- and under-allocated (Smith, 1974). These questions are still relevant. If distributions are not equitable, blaming them on institutional racism is not sufficient. We need to understand why they are that way (Lineberry, 1977). We also need to identify the geographical patterns in the distribution.

#### 3.2.2.1 Measuring the Allocation of City Services

Measurement of the distribution of municipal services has gotten a great deal of attention (Jones, 1977; Jones & Kaufman, 1974; Lineberry & Welch, 1974). One approach is to focus on outcomes, such as improved housing quality. However, the interconnected nature of urban systems makes connecting efforts/outputs (housing inspections and violations) to outcomes (housing quality) difficult. These two factors are not alone in determining housing quality. Other factors such as housing age, median household income, building codes, cultural inclination to repair houses, actions by other governmental agencies at state and federal levels, and other housing programs also affect housing quality (Jones, 1977).

The distributional approach avoids the issues associated with focusing on outcomes by measuring the level of effort expended on providing services (Jones, 1977; Lineberry & Welch, 1974). Several approaches have been suggested for quantifying governmental effort. Two use demand as the denominator: one uses effort relative to potential demand and the other effort relative to expressed demand. Two others focus on quality: input quality and service delivery quality (from the consumer's perspective). Table 1 provides a few examples of measures. Lineberry and Welch (1974) propose that indicators of service delivery quality are the best for distributional research because they directly reflect agency activity and decision-making. They also represent important resident concerns.

#### 3.2.2.2 Explaining the Allocation of City Services

Up to this point, the provision of services has been treated as if each agency is in control of how services are provided. However, there are several internal and

**Table 1** Example variables for measuring the level of effort expended on city services

| Concepts | Specific measures |
|---|---|
| Indicators of input quantity (relative to potential demand) | Patrol officers / Population<br>Fire hydrants / Miles of streets<br>Library books / Population |
| Indicators of input quantity (relative to expressed demand) | Patrol officers / Calls for service<br>Fire trucks / Calls for service<br>Library books / Books borrowed |
| Indicators of input quality | Caliber of police officers (training, experience)<br>Quality of recreational facilities (swimming pools, tennis courts, etc.)<br>High-intensity streetlights / Total streetlights |
| Indicators of service delivery quality (from the consumer's perspective) | Average police response time (to various types of calls for assistance)<br>Missed trash and garbage collections / Total collections<br>Smoothness of streets |

**Note:** Table contents adapted from Lineberry and Welch (1974).

external sources that influence the distribution of services. First, policy decisions within the governmental agency affect service provision (Jones, 1977: 300–301; Lineberry, 1977). For example, policies set the rules that govern regularized service provision. Most often, bureaucratic decision rules reflect professional standards. Second, service delivery can also be influenced by a variety of other external sources of input such as residents via complaints, politicians, wealthy individuals, and interest groups. The most significant of these are the resident complaints, collected in the USA via 311 systems, which now drive a large proportion of service delivery.

### 3.2.2.3 Patterns in Service Provision by Local Governments

Early studies of service distribution predominantly found unpatterned inequality (DeHoog, 1997; Lineberry, 1977). The services were not distributed equally but neither were they systematically unequal. Thus, the research failed to consistently uncover the anticipated links to race and class. However, some studies uncovered service patterns that favored minority and low-income areas such as libraries (Mladenka & Hill, 1977), recreational services (Lineberry, 1977; Mladenka & Hill, 1977). Other studies found that the distribution of services favored white and higher-income areas in regard to recreational services (Mladenka, 1989), lower litter amounts (Antunes & Plumlee, 1977), more sanitation services (Boyle & Jacobs, 1982), less prevalence of open ditches (Antunes & Plumlee, 1977), higher street-maintenance expenditures (Levy et al., 1975), more police services (Boyle & Jacobs, 1982; Cingranelli, 1981), and more fire services (Boyle & Jacobs, 1982; Cingranelli, 1981). Yet another study focusing on enforcement of housing-code violations found that complaints in poorer neighborhoods were more likely to result in formal citations than complaints in middle-class areas (Nivola, 1978). However, a study of Chicago building inspectors discovered that they issued most of their code violations to landlords and wealthy homeowners (Bartram, 2019). Overall, the evidence to date offers no consistent story about the provision of services by local government.

There are several potential explanations for this variability in research findings. One is simply that urban systems are complex, and the distribution of services varies from city to city (Rich, 1979). Another, more plausible explanation is that the variability in findings is due to the relatively rudimentary analysis that was common half a century ago. A third concerns the lack of attention paid to analysis of the inherent spatial dimensions in service provision (Hero, 1986). Geographical issues received greater attention beginning in the early 1980s (McLafferty, 1984; McLafferty & Ghosh, 1982; Talen & Anselin, 1998). These authors noted problems with using a correlation coefficient (McLafferty, 1984; McLafferty & Ghosh, 1982) and demonstrated how measures of accessibility can affect the conclusions drawn from study results (Talen & Anselin, 1998).

A final, important subtext in service distribution research is how it relates to unintended effects of bureaucratic decision rules. Examples of bureaucratic decision rules that affect the amount of city services allocated to places are:

(1) Library resources are allocated based on circulation rates. Since reader levels tend to be correlated with social class, libraries in wealthier and whiter areas get more library resources (Mladenka & Hill, 1977).

(2) Repairs to neighborhood streets are prioritized if a resident complains. Residents in higher-income neighborhoods call in complaints more often, so streets in those neighborhoods are repaired more quickly (Antunes & Plumlee, 1977; Levy et al., 1975).

(3)  Jones and colleagues (1978) identified three decision rules related to trash pickup frequency. Picking up garbage once a week, every week is a neutral decision rule. Trucks and crews allocated by the amount of garbage is a decision rule that favors areas that produce more garbage, such as wealthy areas. Providing additional resources to city centers is a decision rule that favors the businesses and residences on those streets.

These rules are used to allocate finite resources and do not explicitly discriminate by race or class, but they do have consequences that result in unequal distribution to different areas (Mladenka, 1989) and unequal impacts.

### 3.2.3 Linking Government Services to Crime: Theory and Empirical Evidence

Criminological theories offer a framework for explaining how government services are likely to be linked to crime. Recent work has demonstrated a connection between the routine provision of those services and crime. This section begins with theory and then covers the rather meager evidence-base.

### 3.2.3.1 Theoretical Framework

Several theories under the rubric of environmental criminology are relevant to linking the quality of the urban backcloth to crime. The rational choice perspective provides a blueprint for modeling the decision-making process of crime commission (Clarke & Cornish, 1985). It provides the foundation for understanding criminal decision-making in both crime pattern theory (CPT) and routine activity (RA) theory. Basically, individuals weigh perceived risks and anticipated benefits using bounded rationality (i.e., make decisions using the information at hand).

Crime pattern theory articulates four dimensions of crime – legal, offending, target, and place – and centers characteristics of the urban backcloth and how those characteristics influence the decision to commit a crime (Brantingham & Brantingham, 1984, 1991 [1981]). The urban backcloth encompasses the physical, social, economic, and cultural aspects of a situation. Land use and transportation routes structure the number of people in a place. The roles of people at a place as well as the characteristics of the places in which a crime occurs are very important in understanding crime in CPT. Routine activity theory (Cohen & Felson, 1979) shares several of the same elements as CPT but explicitly introduces the guardianship role. The presence of guardians increases the riskiness of a situation. Extensions to the original conceptualization of guardianship (Eck, 1995; Felson, 1995) have produced more nuanced and comprehensive articulations of guardianship.

Two of the most well-developed extensions of guardianship in RA theory are place management theory (Madensen & Eck, 2013) and super-controllers (Sampson et al., 2010). Place management theory is described in detail in Section 3.1 of this Element. Super-controllers are people who control place managers (Sampson et al., 2010). Licensing agencies, inspectors, and other government employees whose job it is to enforce civil and municipal codes are super-controllers. They can alter the behavior of place managers through their authority to issue violations and revoke licenses.

Together these theories make clear the importance of the quality of the built environment in reducing crime opportunity. Local government services directly influence the quality of the built environment and the effectiveness of place management. Several police-led strategies have harnessed the power of local government agencies to reduce crime.

### 3.2.3.2 Police-Led Strategies Leveraging Local Government Services

Place-focused policing strategies including neighborhood team policing (Bloch & Specht, 1973; Sherman et al., 1973), third-party policing (Buerger & Mazerolle, 1998), and PNIs (Herold et al., 2020) draw from environmental criminology and combine the identification of problem places by the police with careful fieldwork and community input to develop responses. Coordinated local government response typically relies upon regulation, in the form of code enforcement, to address issues.

Neighborhood team policing (Bloch & Specht, 1973; Sherman et al., 1973) emphasizes interaction with city agencies and the community, the geographic stability of patrol assignment to small areas, and intentional and intensive communication among team members to solve community problems.

Third-party policing coordinates the actions of place managers and those taken by representatives of local government (Buerger & Mazerolle, 1998). Such actions leverage ownership powers and the regulatory components of civil law, respectively. Third-party policing usually begins after the police have analyzed a crime problem and decided that they require the assistance of an authority outside the criminal law purview to address it (Buerger, 2007)

Place network investigations (Herold et al., 2020), discussed in Section 3.1, use a multi-step strategy that combines hot-spot identification with intensive fieldwork by crime analysts and sworn officers to identify the networks of places that in combination provide the infrastructure to support criminal enterprise. Crime–place networks can involve four types of place: crime sites (locations of crime), convergent settings (public places where offenders meet), comfort spaces (private places where offenders meet and store supplies), and corrupting spots (places that encourage crime that occurs elsewhere). Place–network investigation focuses the attention of place managers and government agencies (typically via code enforcement) on those shadow places in the network. It requires the active participation of relevant government agencies to successfully address the structures that support criminal activity.

All three of these strategies are police-led approaches that focus on cooling crime hot spots. The success of these efforts suggests that *routinely* addressing the urban backcloth issues by, for example, enforcing municipal codes, picking up trash, repairing potholes, and providing recreation programs can help local governments prevent the formation of crime hot spots.

### 3.2.3.3 Empirical Evidence Supporting the Role of City Services in Addressing the Built Environment–Crime Connection

A variety of different routine local government functions have been linked to crime reductions. Probably the strongest evidence exists for regulatory efforts. Specifically, efforts to remediate vacant lots and abandoned housing have frequently been associated with reductions in crime. Remediation or demolition of abandoned buildings (Kondo et al., 2015; Stacy, 2018) and remediation of vacant lots have been linked to lower numbers of crime and gun violence incidents (Branas et al., 2011, 2018; Moyer et al., 2019).[7]

Local governments can apply a variety of tools such as code enforcement, tax foreclosure, eminent domain, and exterior improvements (Accordino & Johnson, 2000). One study provided grants to homeowners to fund structural repairs. Block faces on which homeowners received grants experienced a 21.9 percent decrease in crime and block faces with higher numbers of grant homes had larger crime reductions (South et al., 2021). Enforcement in the form of demolition has been associated with a 5 percent crime decrease in the area up to 1,000 feet from the property (Wheeler et al., 2018).

The City of Philadelphia offers a particularly compelling example of the systematic use of a housing ordinance. In 2011, Philadelphia enacted the Doors and Windows Ordinance. The ordinance required that doors and windows in all abandoned properties were working and kept locked by the owner. City inspectors were sent to inspect all vacant buildings. Those with open windows or doors were cited via a pink sticker on the door and a letter. An evaluation found that installing doors and windows in abandoned homes reduced assaults and gun assaults around the buildings (Kondo et al., 2015).

A study of six different cities found that increases in building permits and code enforcement were significantly negatively related to all crime, violent

---

[7] But see Han and Helm (2023) for conflicting evidence regarding demolitions.

crime, property crime, disorder crime, and other crime (Tillyer et al., 2023). But the size of the relationship varied by crime type and by city. Property crime had the highest effect sizes. Rather than displacement, a diffusion of benefits (Clarke & Weisburd, 1994) effect was seen related to code enforcement in all six cities and to building permits in five of the six cities. Additionally, there was a strong persistence effect from year to year.

These few studies provide growing evidence for the effectiveness of regulatory city services at reducing crime. However, local government provides a wide variety of services that directly affect the quality of the built environment. More research is needed that directly and systematically examines services' effects on crime.

### 3.2.4 Future Directions of Leveraging Municipal Levers for Reducing Crime at Places

This section outlines the connection between local government services that maintain the quality of the built environment and crime. There are a variety of different local government services that contribute to the quality of the built environment and thus are likely to affect crime. Code enforcement is the only one that has been systematically examined at the micro-level of street segment or census block group. Table 2 provides some examples of service provision measures that could be developed at each unit of analysis. Many other types of service could also be examined.

Most of the work examining local government provision of services was completed in the 1960s and 1970s using rudimentary analysis methods and large geographies. Since then there have been significant advances in data availability, methods, and statistical techniques. Today, open data portals contain a great deal of data documenting the provision of services, although the lack of comprehensive metadata is a barrier to their effective use. Improvements in methods and statistical techniques include the ability to use street rather than Euclidean ("as the crow flies") distance measures, the use of micro-level units of analysis, and the explicit modeling of spatial autocorrelation, spatial spillovers, and spatial externalities (see discussions in McLafferty, 1984; McLafferty & Ghosh, 1982; Talen & Anselin, 1998). The integration of these more sophisticated methods and statistical models at micro-levels is needed to investigate these relationships and produce more robust findings.

Emphasizing the importance of local government service provision as a crime prevention strategy offers potential advantages. First, it is a fundamentally practical approach that views public safety as emerging from the contributions of various urban backcloth attributes. Second, equity in built environment

**Table 2** Measures of service provision

| Service | Street segment | Census block group |
|---|---|---|
| Code enforcement (housing, nuisance, fire) | Number of code enforcement inspections* | Density of code enforcement inspections** |
| | Number of code enforcement citations issued* | Density of code enforcement citations issued** |
| | Number of closed actions* | Number of closed actions** |
| Dumping remediation | Number of cleanups per mile | Density of cleanups per area |
| Garbage pickup | Frequency of pickup | Frequency of pickup |
| | Number of missed pickups by total possible pickups | Number of missed pickups by total possible pickups |
| Graffiti remediation | Number of remediations by mile | Density of remediations by area |
| Road maintenance: repaving | Years since last repaved | Average years since last repaved (across all streets) |
| Road maintenance: repair | Number of repairs completed by number of complaints | Number of repairs completed by number of complaints |
| | Number of potholes repaired by number of complaints | Number of potholes repaired by number of complaints |
| | Average time to repair after complaint | Average time to repair after complaint |
| Pavement rating | Pavement quality rating | Average pavement quality rating |
| Sidewalks | Percentage of street with sidewalks | Percentage of road miles with sidewalks |
| Streetlights | Proportion of street lit | Proportion of streets lit |
| | Number of streetlights by street length | Number of streetlights per mile of road |

**Notes:** *by mile or total housing units; **by area or total housing units.

quality can be addressed by focusing on service provision. Some have discussed the potential for code enforcement to reinforce existing patterns of racial and economic inequality (Lieb, 2018). However, those concerns are not borne out by the research evidence. Third, it could stimulate the routine tracking of the provision of services to develop a more nuanced understanding of the mechanisms underpinning the built environment–crime connection. The time for more research is now.

## 4 Expanding the Focus of Crime-and-Place Research

### 4.1 The Importance of Focusing on Rural Places

Social processes within communities have been studied for over 100 years and, while a newer phenomenon, the law of crime concentration (Weisburd, 2015) is also well-established.[8] However, the vast majority of these bodies of research are based on data from urban or, less often, suburban communities. This is a significant limitation because a substantial minority of people in the United States and worldwide live in rural areas. Although the rural population is declining, the World Bank (n.d.) classifies just under 45 percent of the world's population as rural, and 20 percent of the US population – 60 million people – live in rural areas, which account for 97 percent of the country's land mass (America Counts, 2017; Ratcliffe et al., 2016). Notably, there is no consistent definition of "rural." The World Bank uses individual countries' classifications to determine the rural population, and different US government agencies use different approaches. The US Census Bureau defines rural as simply "what is not urban" (Ratcliffe et al., 2016: 1), which in turn is determined by population size and density, land use, and density of buildings or residents. In general, administratively defined places containing fewer than 2,500 people are considered nonurban.

There is a stereotype, at least in the United States, that "urban" is synonymous with "crime-ridden" and "rural" is synonymous with "safe." While in absolute numbers there are more crimes in urban areas, simply by virtue of population size, this assumption is incorrect. "Rural" is not a monolith. For many people the term conjures up images of bucolic farmland and happy, close-knit communities, but rural populations as defined by the government exist in places as diverse as the Appalachian Mountains, the far suburbs of major cities like Atlanta, and the Mojave Desert. These populations face a range of problems that also exist in cities, and they face a higher risk of some crimes than their urban counterparts on a per-population basis (Abraham & Ceccato, 2022;

---

[8] Section 4.1 was drafted by Charlotte Gill.

Kanewske, 2023; Kuhns et al., 2007; Weisheit et al., 2006). Overall, the lack of attention paid to the nuances of rural communities in crime-and-place research means that criminologists have neglected a nontrivial portion of the population.[9]

This is not simply an academic oversight. Given the extent to which the evidence-base for effective place-based crime prevention relies on the theoretical and empirical contributions of the crime-and-place literature, it is crucial to examine whether our understanding of crime concentration translates to rural settings. If not, the ability of rural communities to benefit from the development and implementation of effective crime prevention approaches is directly affected. The remainder of this section explores this issue through the lens of two of David Weisburd's key contributions to the crime-and-place field – the concentration of crime at micro-places (specifically street segments) and the relevance of the social context at these places.

### 4.1.1 What Does Micro-place-level Crime Concentration Look Like in Rural Areas?

A handful of studies explore the spatial distribution of crime in larger areas, such as counties, that include rural communities and/or compare rural and urban crime rates (e.g., Ceccato & Dolmen, 2011; Mawby, 2007; Messner et al., 1999; Wells & Weisheit, 2004). However, there are no studies of micro-level patterns of general crime concentration in truly rural settings. Studies of suburban or small city locations do show that crime in these types of place tends to be more concentrated at specific street blocks or segments relative to concentration levels in more urbanized areas (Gill et al., 2017; Weisburd, 2015). Several recent studies have also examined the micro-level concentration of a specific type of police call for service – mental health crisis calls – at rural or suburban-rural locations (Koziarski, 2021, 2023). Taken together, this small body of literature supports the idea that in nonurban areas the "bandwidth," as Weisburd (2015) describes it, of crime concentration may be much narrower than it is in large urban cities. It is therefore possible that as areas get more rural, crime may become even more highly concentrated at micro-places.

A key challenge for researchers, which may partially explain the lack of empirical research, is how to measure and conceptualize rural crime concentration. The concept of street segments is tied to an urban-centric (and distinctly North American) vision of street layout and land use, in which large cities are

---

[9] A number of scholars are doing important research on rural crime issues (see, e.g., Donnermeyer, 2016); however, rural settings are poorly represented in the crime concentration and evidence-based crime prevention literature specifically.

laid out on a grid and street segments are somewhat uniform in length. This is important from both a measurement and a theoretical perspective. The relative uniformity of urban street segments allows for easier comparisons between units; one could argue that the longer the street segment, the more opportunities for crime, simply because there may be more buildings, more pedestrian and/or vehicle traffic, and so on. Furthermore, Weisburd and colleagues (2012, 2016a, 2023b; also see Kuen et al., 2022) conceptualized street segments as "behavioral settings" in part because, in a typical urban city, it is usually possible to see and experience social activities on the entire block at once. In other words, a person's routine activities and the social context in which they operate are likely to shape their behavior and experiences.

To illustrate the variety of street layouts in rural settings, three examples are presented of street segments and hot spots of youth crime in Bell, Clay, and Harlan Counties in rural Southeastern Kentucky, United States. This information was gathered as part of a Bureau of Justice Assistance-funded grant that was active from 2015 to 2018, in which we identified hot spots of juvenile and youth crime in the three counties.[10] While the goal of this project was to identify locations for intervention rather than a primary empirical analysis of rural crime concentration, these counties provide a practical example of the realities of rural crime. Bell, Clay, Harlan, and five other counties in the region comprise the Kentucky Highlands Promise Zone (PZ), so designated as part of an Obama White House initiative to address poverty and economic decline (Hud Exchange, n.d.). The entire PZ has a population of just over 200,000 in 3,000 square miles, and no towns larger than 10,000 people. These communities have been severely affected by the recent opioid crisis, and entrenched crime problems include substance use, manufacturing, and trafficking, as well as crimes related to maintaining a drug dependency, such as shoplifting and other theft (Meglen & Gill, 2020).

Figure 1 shows that some "larger" rural towns have street layouts that resemble urban areas. This map depicts youth-crime hot spots in Middlesboro, one of the largest towns in Bell County with a population of approximately 9,700. Much of the downtown area is laid out on a grid, as in larger cities, although it is surrounded by less-uniform street segments in the outlying residential neighborhoods. Here, the hot spots we identified look somewhat more "traditional" in that there are several areas where crime is more heavily concentrated. For example, Segment C on the map comprised some commercial properties, including gas

---

[10] See Gentry et al. (2018), Gill et al. (2015), and Meglen and Gill (2020) for more details on how we identified these hot spots using ArcGIS. In the examples that follow, "youth crime" refers to crimes recorded by the Kentucky State Police that involved youths aged eighteen to twenty-five as suspects or victims.

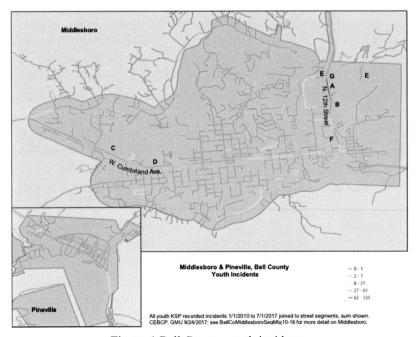

**Figure 1** Bell County youth incidents.

stations, restaurants, and small retail stores, as well as a middle and high school (which likely drove the higher rate of crime involving younger people). Over 200 crimes were recorded there between January 2010 and May 2018 (including crimes involving juveniles and adults), almost half of which were larceny/theft. Segment A had an extremely heavy concentration of crime, with over 2,000 incidents involving people of all ages recorded there in the same time period. There is a Walmart store, a mall, and a number of other commercial and retail properties at this location, and over three-quarters of all incidents were larceny/theft offenses.

Figure 2 depicts Harlan, the county seat of Harlan County. This is a much smaller town than Middlesboro, with a population of only 1,500. However, along with Cumberland, a city of 2,000 to the northeast, it is one of the main population centers in the county. Despite being one of the larger towns in the county, there is much less uniformity in the length and layout of street segments here compared to Middlesboro. Nonetheless, the "hot" segments are still small enough to potentially represent behavior settings and crime is still highly concentrated at a handful of very small segments. As in Middlesboro, Segment A is a commercial area with a Walmart and a few other small retail stores. There were 268 recorded incidents at this segment between January 2010 and March 2018, of which around two-thirds were larceny/theft offenses.

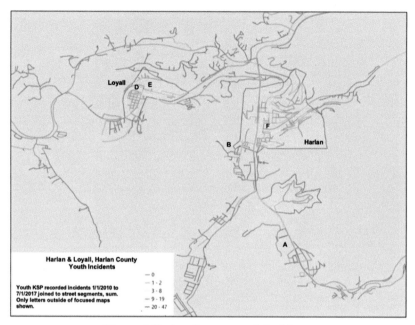

**Figure 2** Harlan County youth incidents.

Segment B is in a residential neighborhood and comprises a public housing complex and a number of single-family homes. Only forty-eight incidents were recorded here during the same time period, but the concentration on a single street segment is notable and likely reflects the greater population density at the public housing complex (most residences in the area are single-family properties). These incidents included drugs/narcotics, assault, larceny/theft, and burglary offenses.

Figure 3 illustrates how the idea of the street segment as a self-contained behavior setting begins to break down in some rural communities. This map shows the area surrounding Manchester, a town of 1,500 people that is the county seat and the only population center in Clay County. Segment E2, the main highway through the county, is almost 10 miles long. Segments B1 and D1 are very sparsely populated residential areas. Segments E and E1 are close to a hospital and likely represent a "magnet location" for reporting rather than actual crime locations. Segment A is a remote location along a main road, but it features a convenience store, a church, and several open, unsupervised spaces. A total of eighty-three incidents were recorded there by police during the same time period reported above; around two-thirds of these were drugs/narcotics-related.

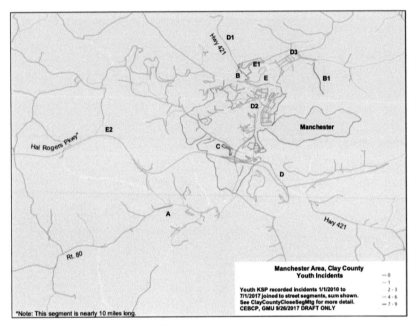

**Figure 3** Clay County youth incidents.

Consistent with prior research, these maps illustrate that crime appears to be very highly concentrated at a small number of street segments in these particular rural towns. However, they also show that street segments may not always be the most appropriate unit of analysis in these types of area. As we reach higher levels of "rurality" (from a land use or street layout perspective), we may start to lose the empirical and theoretical benefits of using this unit of analysis, suggesting a need to explore other measures (Lee & Eck, 2019). Several statistical approaches exist to assess crime concentration under these conditions. The Gini coefficient assesses inequality in a population and has been adapted by crime-and-place researchers to report and summarize the level of crime concentration at a place. Bernasco and Steenbeek's (2017) generalized version performs well when there are more places than crimes, as would likely be the case in a rural area where crime incidents may be sparse. Similarly, the location quotient (LQ) assesses the over- or underrepresentation of criminal activity relative to the broader geographic area (Andresen, 2007, 2013; Andresen et al., 2009; Groff, 2011). An extension of this measure that adapts the LQ along linear features such as roads (Wuschke et al., 2021) could be particularly valuable for assessing crime concentration along the long street segments we saw in Clay County (Figure 3). Ratcliffe (2005) used nearest-neighbor comparisons and ranking to identify clustering of crime in Australia, which also has expansive rural locations that may not be amenable to traditional methods of assessing crime concentration.

However, a limitation of these statistical approaches is that they generate only a single value that tells us about overall crime concentration. This is useful for comparing between different jurisdictions but does not provide specific information about the location or the nature of the hot spot. The power of the street segment lies in its utility as a unit for practical prevention. As some of the previous examples show, even if the segment does not perfectly operate as a self-contained activity space, the ability to determine what businesses or residential locations exist at these hot spots opens up possibilities for intervention.

The concept of "risky facilities" (Eck et al., 2007) offers a feasible alternative to the street segment with similar benefits. Risky facilities are places that have a specific function (e.g., bars, apartment buildings, stores) and generate disproportionately high levels of crime relative to other facilities of the same type. They are often nonresidential or "proprietary places," as John Eck describes in this Element. Some researchers have suggested that "hot" street segments may simply reflect an amalgamation of risky facilities on the block (Lee et al., 2022; Tillyer & Walter, 2019; Wilcox & Eck, 2011). This fits well with the rural context, where facilities such as shopping areas tend to be concentrated in just a few street segments due to low population density and sparsely used land (e.g., Townsley et al., 2000). Birks et al. (2023) found that opportunities for different types of crime in Australia were more dispersed in larger cities where there is a more expansive urban spread, whereas in rural areas with highly concentrated population centers suitable opportunities are limited to a smaller area.

Along these lines, Walmart stores accounted for two of the hot spots in Bell and Harlan Counties. This may simply be because more people tend to congregate at Walmart because it is a central shopping location for the county. However, Walmart specifically has been studied as an example of a "risky facility" because of its lax approach to loss prevention (Zidar et al., 2018). Thus, this distinction between hot street segments and risky facilities could be an important avenue to explore in rural areas. Within street segments, regardless of their length, can we pinpoint specific addresses and/or types of place that are generating a majority of the crime and find creative ways to intervene there? Crime concentration could be extremely sensitive to changes in these facilities and the level of place management, which could also be manipulated in crime prevention efforts.

### 4.1.2 Social Disorganization and Crime

A further challenge to urban-centric thinking about crime concentration is the lack of evidence to support social disorganization as an explanation for crime in rural areas. Weisburd and his colleagues have been instrumental in demonstrating the relationship between opportunity and the social context at the microplace level in cities (Weisburd et al., 2012, 2014a, 2020, 2021b). Levels of social disorganization (including population turnover and poverty), social ties and cohesion, and collective efficacy all affect people's behavior, interactions with each other, and willingness or capacity to act as guardians who (directly or indirectly) protect potential targets in the space. Even at the street block level, "small-scale social systems" (Wicker, 1987: 614; see also Taylor, 1997) operate, again driven by environmental factors, and levels of social disorganization can vary in the same way as crime from one block to the next. Standing patterns of behavior develop around these defined places, and people who use the space take on certain roles and norms. The interactions and relationships between individuals and institutions within these spaces help to develop informal social controls that regulate behavior; crime results when these controls break down (Bursik & Grasmick, 1993; Taylor, 1997; Weisburd, 2012; Weisburd et al., 2015a).

Despite the stereotype that rural areas are idyllic and safe compared to urban areas, rural residents face a range of problems that have traditionally been linked to social disorganization-based explanations for crime in cities. The counties with the highest poverty levels in the United States are heavily clustered in nonmetropolitan areas, and 80 percent of "persistent child poverty" counties – those with consistent child poverty rates of 20 percent or more over thirty years – are rural (Schaefer et al., 2016; see also Economic Research Service, 2023). It is arguably still socially acceptable to label members of communities like those in Appalachian Kentucky as "hillbillies" or "white trash" and to discriminate against them accordingly. These communities have been ravaged by the effects of prescription opioid addiction, which is compounded by stereotyping from the outside and isolation within. However, research at the county level shows limited support for the relationship between social disorganization and crime in rural communities (Kaylen & Pridemore, 2012, 2013; compare with Bouffard & Muftić, 2006). On the other hand, one study that incorporates both street-segment- and neighborhood-level predictors of social disorganization and routine activities perspectives finds support for elements of both theories (Jones & Pridemore, 2019). These mixed findings suggest that the mechanisms that produce rural disorganization may differ from those that produce urban disorganization.

Relatedly, some research also shows that the social features that tend to protect against crime are stronger in rural areas than in cities, but this does not necessarily translate into lower crime rates. Economic migration aside, population turnover in some rural communities may be lower than in fast-paced urban settings. While the population has decreased significantly in regions like Appalachia as traditional industries like coal mining have declined, those who remain are likely to have been born and grown up in the area. Many are strongly opposed to the idea of leaving their communities and derive feelings of safety from their proximity to family or known neighbors (Kanewske, 2023). Thus, standing patterns of behavior still develop and informal social control can be exerted through relationships between families and institutions, such as schools and churches, that bring geographically isolated residents together. Yet, while we would expect these factors to increase collective efficacy, which Weisburd and colleagues demonstrate is protective against crime in an urban setting, some research from rural areas suggests that high levels of informal social control may in fact facilitate crime, as close-knit community members protect each other (Barclay et al., 2004; DeKeseredy, 1990; Donnermeyer & DeKeseredy, 2014; Jobes et al., 2004; Keyes et al., 2014). Conversely, the relative lack of anonymity in rural areas may discourage potential offenders. Nonetheless, research suggests that social trust/capital and collective action may be more important protective factors in rural communities (Chilenski et al., 2015; Deller & Deller, 2010; Lee & Thomas, 2010).

### 4.1.3 Conclusion

The conclusion that more research is needed on the questions raised in this section is obvious, so we end this section with some thoughts about how such research might be done and subsequently leveraged to add to the evidence-base on crime prevention in rural communities. The issue of how to intervene at the hot spots we identified in Southeastern Kentucky became a central challenge of our work that related to both of the issues identified here – the concentration of crime around risky facilities and making sense of how the social context operates in rural communities. As noted earlier, place management can be challenging at large chain stores like Walmart, as employees often need corporate approval to participate in programs and there may be rules and policies around reporting crime that inflate the likelihood of reporting at these locations. As Zidar et al. (2018) showed, corporate policies may even be driving crime rates up through a lack of interest or investment in in-house loss prevention.

In some remote locations, there may not be opportunities to intervene at all. Many young residents we interviewed in Kentucky identified abandoned mountaintop strip mines (a type of mine where the top of the mountain is leveled or "stripped" to reveal the coal underneath) as potential hot spots, because they are unsupervised and difficult to access by police (which means problems do not show up in official crime data), and provide a hidden location for groups of young people to use alcohol and drugs (Gentry et al., 2018; Meglen & Gill, 2020). Increasing police patrol and holding community events on the mountaintop are not practical solutions to these issues. Instead, we came up with the idea of identifying "bright spots" – places in the community that could serve to draw people away from areas where crime opportunities exist – as an alternative to hot spots (Meglen & Gill, 2020). Bright spots are not necessarily lower-crime areas; rather, they are places where there are opportunities for fun activities and community building, drawing on the idea of collective action. This brings a new angle to assessing rural crime concentration – where are the *opportunities for intervention*?

Identifying rural crime concentration, the mechanisms underlying it, and the opportunities for intervention may also involve going beyond quantitative assessments of crime rates and engaging in qualitative work as described in Section 4.3 of this Element. Cognitive mapping exercises with community members could identify both hot and bright spots, and validate or expand on hot locations identified through police data (e.g., Hibdon, 2011). For example, in Kentucky we conducted an informal cognitive mapping process in which we asked community members to study a map of their county and highlight the areas they believed to be hot and bright spots. They also described the possible factors that might draw potential offenders away from a specific hot spot and toward a bright spot. Similarly, in a study of an urban community, Gill et al. (2016) asked community members to validate the hot spots that were identified via police reports (Gill et al., 2016). They not only asked community members whether the locations made sense as focus areas but also tapped into deep community knowledge about what might be driving crime at those places. Overall, there is a strong imperative to center the voices and expertise of rural residents in the further development of this work, as they have been neglected in our field for too long.

## 4.2 Staking Out Health Outcomes as an Important Part of the Criminology of Place

While the study of crime events and why crime concentrates in space and time is well-established in criminology, much of what we know about crime hot spots is limited to measures of land use and the built environment, and we know much less about the social context of these places.[11] A multidisciplinary approach

---

[11]  Section 4.2 was drafted by Clair V. Uding.

drawn from the foundation laid by crime-and-place research would be useful to enable examining other social problems in these places, particularly health, and could provide important insights about the relationships between crime, health, and place. In turn, criminal justice and health practitioners could be better informed when working with people impacted by crime because of where they reside. Before discussing future directions for research and practice on crime, place, and health, it is helpful to provide some perspective on how research and policies have begun to understand the interconnectedness of crime and health.

### 4.2.1 The Intersection of Criminology, Criminal Justice, and Health

The intersection of criminology, criminal justice, and health has gained more attention in recent decades, in both research and practice. It is now accepted that public health and criminal justice practitioners typically work with similar disadvantaged populations, and that offending populations tend to have poorer health than the general public (Binswanger et al., 2007; Farrington, 1995; Rosen et al., 2008; Shepard et al., 2004). Public health and geography research in urban settings has also started to examine the relationship between neighborhood violence and health outcomes, particularly as it relates to characteristics of the environment (Baranyi et al., 2021; Meyer et al., 2014; O'Campo et al., 2015; Phelan et al., 2004; Zhang et al., 2011). Nonetheless, the understanding of crime and health has largely been kept as distinct disciplines and less attention has been paid to the overlap of these areas of social life.

Epidemiological criminology is a newer paradigm aimed at understanding health and crime from a multidisciplinary approach. It is defined as "an epistemological and etiological integration of theories, methods, practices, and technologies used in public health and criminal justice that incorporates the broader interdisciplinary framework of epidemiology and criminology" (Akers et al., 2013: 48; also see Potter & Akers, 2010).[12] Akers, Potter, and Hill (2013) highlight several criminological theories used to understand deviance and crime that would be useful for epidemiology and public health, noting that "the recognition of criminological contributions to understanding risky behaviors is almost completely absent from public health epidemiology" (p. 52) and that "criminology is an ideal model for interdisciplinary science" (p. 53). Alternatively, criminology focuses on a narrow number of outcomes related to delinquent and criminal behavior, paying less attention to other co-occurring problems, such as the impact of crime on health outcomes. When thinking about rehabilitation or preventing recidivism, these other

---

[12] Epidemiology is an area of medicine that studies "the incidence, distribution, and possible control of diseases and other factors relating to health" (Oxford English Dictionary, 2010).

factors, like health, can impact the offender's success and pose challenges for practitioners working with offending populations.

The theoretical application of criminological theories can range from identifying the similar risk factors for criminal involvement and poor health, such as low socioeconomic status, to understanding risky and offending behaviors that put individuals at risk for health problems. Health risks posed by engaging in certain crimes like intravenous drug use or sex work, or being a victim of crime, are more obvious and can present significant challenges and concerns for public health and criminal justice workers alike. The study of corrections and health outcomes among incarcerated and formally incarcerated individuals has also gained more attention over the years, as well as the reframing of gun violence as a public health crisis (Bauchner et al., 2017). Yet, much of this research is focused at the individual level and the study of crime and health outcomes from an ecological perspective has been more limited.

### 4.2.2 Health Disparities at Microgeographic Places

At the macrogeographic level, it is becoming well-established that neighborhood characteristics associated with crime, such as socioeconomic disadvantage and residential segregation, are also linked to several negative health outcomes (Browning & Cagney, 2003; Curry et al., 2008; Diez Roux & Mair, 2010). However, due to data limitations, we know little about the residents who live in places with high concentrations of crime, particularly in regard to people's health and mental health. In the study of microgeographic places and crime, the roles of the physical environment and opportunity are key features through which to understand crime events and patterning (Brantingham & Brantingham, 1993; MacDonald, 2015). Similarly, the role of the built environment and land use, such as vacant lots and green spaces, as well the walkability of a neighborhood and its implications for health have also gained more empirical attention in the areas of public health and geography (Branas et al., 2011; Garvin et al., 2013; Gianfredi et al., 2021; Lorenc et al., 2012; South et al., 2015, 2018).

The main limitation of health research at place is the broader neighborhood perspective and the aggregation of crime or health measures to larger units of analysis, such as census tracts. Health is rarely studied in the context of crime hot spots. Just as high concentrations of crime at small places can drive up the crime rate for a neighborhood (Weisburd et al., 2012), the small pockets of people living in these crime hot spots may deal with significantly more health problems and/or obstacles in accessing and participating in health and treatment services. Like neighborhood research on crime, variation in health outcomes within neighborhoods is likely masked by aggregating to larger ecological units of analysis. Levels of physical and social disorder in neighborhoods can impact people's use of space and walkability due to concerns around safety, which has indirect impacts on health (Gómez et al., 2004; McDonald, 2008), but disorder, like crime, is not evenly distributed across a neighborhood. At the neighborhood level, people can avoid streets and places with high levels of disorder to continue to engage in physical activity, and the stressors of living in a disadvantaged neighborhood may not be felt as greatly compared to someone who lives on a disadvantaged, high-crime street. As such, living in a crime hot spot may have a more direct impact on people's health and mental health. While communities are small in comparison to international and national-level research on health and the spread of diseases, microgeographic places are an important unit of analysis that is worth pursuing in public health research and policy. The quality of health programs targeted at disadvantaged communities has been a central focus of public health initiatives to address health disparities, but this may be too broad a geographic area to enable delivery of programs and services, thus failing to target those with the most need.

### 4.2.3 Hot Spots and Health Disparities: Empirical Data

In a study on crime hot spots in Baltimore, Weisburd and White (2019) found significant differences in health outcomes across different types of street segment with residents of crime hot spots reporting more health problems and limitations. In particular, there were higher rates of asthma, high blood pressure, and lung disease among residents living in hot spots; residents of hot spots were more likely to rate their health as poor or very poor; and the impact of health problems on completing daily activities like carrying groceries and bending over was greater among residents in hot spots (see Weisburd & White, 2019). These findings were based on one wave of survey data collection that took place in 2013 and 2014, but Weisburd et al. (2011) collected two additional waves of data, one in 2015 and the other in 2017, which allow us to probe more deeply into the hot spot–health relationship and also to see whether such a relationship remains stable over time. As such, we look to see if there were similar disparities in health problems across street segments.

Residential surveys were conducted on 449 street segments in Baltimore City, categorized by levels of crime, using calls for service. There were 47 cold streets, 100 cool spots, 120 drug hot spots, 127 violent hot spots, and 55 combined-drug-and-violent-crime hot spots.[13] In the second wave of data collection in 2015 a

---

[13] The sampling strategy involved a multi-stage cluster sampling procedure beginning with a sample of 25,045 street segments as the primary unit of analysis in Baltimore. Police calls for service obtained from the Baltimore City Police Department in 2012 were used as the measure of

total of 3,615 surveys were completed, and there were 3,141 completed surveys in the third wave. The survey asked several questions related to general quality of health, health diagnoses, the impact of health on daily activities, and mental health measures of depression and post-traumatic stress disorder (PTSD).[14] It is important to note that self-assessed health measures ranging from general health to diagnoses and symptomology are fairly subjective and influenced by a variety of factors such as socioeconomic status, cultural differences, and other characteristics like occupation, as well as the survey method of data collection (Crossley & Kennedy, 2002; Johnston et al., 2009; Zajacova & Dowd, 2011). The same can also be said of perceptions of crime and fear of crime (see Ambrey et al., 2014); therefore, measurement issues related to these concepts should not be discounted when examining the complex relationship between the social and physical environment of communities and place, crime, and health.

### 4.2.3.1 Overall Health Status and Quality of Health

The individual health measures from the survey are presented in Tables 3 and 4, for Waves 2 and 3, respectively. For overall health status, respondents were asked to describe their health as "very good," "good," "average," "poor," or "very poor." Consistent with the findings from Weisburd and White (2019), there are significant differences in overall health status in both Waves 2 and 3. On the cold streets 4.5 percent of residents indicated that they had poor or very poor health, compared to 10.3 percent of residents in combined hot spots in Wave 2.

There were four items used to measure quality of health: whether the individual feels they get sick more than other people, if they often feel worn out, if they expect their health to get worse, and whether they think their health is excellent. The findings also align with the first wave, particularly in Wave 2, where residents in hot spots were more likely to report that they get sick more than other people

---

crime and geocoded to the street centerline to create counts of crime for service for every street segment in Baltimore. The initial threshold for violent and drug crime was eighteen drug calls and nineteen violence-related calls, respectively (approximately the top 2.5 percent of segments in the city for each category). Although this was the final threshold for the combined-drug-and-violent-crime hot spots, to meet the sampling goals for streets that were hot spots of violence or hot spots of drug crime the threshold was reduced to seventeen violent calls and sixteen drug calls, respectively (approximately the top 3 percent of all city street segments in that category). We also required that streets evidence drug or violent crime throughout the year by setting a criterion that calls be spread across at least six months. In our sampling frame of residential streets (4,630), 284 were classified as violent-crime hot spots, 248 as drug-crime hot spots, 98 as combined-drug-and-violent-crime hot spots, and 4,000 were comparison street segments.

[14] Survey items were drawn from the National Survey on Drug Use and Health and the Survey of Community, Crime, and Health (US Department of Health and Human Services, 2008; see also Ross & Britt, 1995) and the RAND 36-Item Health Survey and the Patient Health Questionnaire (PHQ-9).

**Table 3** Wave 2 health measures by segment type

| | Street segment type | | | | |
| --- | --- | --- | --- | --- | --- |
| | Cold | Cool | Drug | Violent | Combined |
| | % | % | % | % | % |
| **Overall health status*** (*Very poor/Poor*) | 4.5 | 6.5 | 6.8 | 7.7 | 10.3 |
| **Quality of health (*Mostly true/Definitely true*)** | | | | | |
| You seem to get sick more than other people** | 9.0 | 10.3 | 10.7 | 11.0 | 16.9 |
| You often feel worn out** | 30.3 | 36.1 | 33.3 | 38.1 | 40.7 |
| You expect your health to get worse | 18.3 | 18.2 | 16.3 | 19.8 | 17.6 |
| Your health is excellent*** | 75.8 | 64.3 | 66.5 | 63.7 | 61.1 |
| **Daily activities impacted by health (*A lot*)** | | | | | |
| Bathing or dressing yourself | 1.7 | 2.1 | 2.8 | 2.6 | 1.9 |
| Bending down or kneeling** | 3.9 | 8.6 | 9.6 | 9.0 | 11.9 |
| Doing housework* | 3.2 | 7.1 | 7.5 | 8.1 | 7.7 |
| Carrying groceries | 3.7 | 5.8 | 6.4 | 6.6 | 7.9 |
| Doing strenuous activities*** | 8.0 | 16.0 | 16.8 | 16.9 | 16.9 |

**Table 3** (cont.)

| | Street segment type | | | | |
| --- | --- | --- | --- | --- | --- |
| | Cold | Cool | Drug | Violent | Combined |
| | % | % | % | % | % |
| Climbing one flight of stairs | 3.5 | 7.0 | 7.1 | 7.2 | 8.3 |
| Climbing several flights of stairs*** | 5.8 | 14.5 | 13.7 | 15.8 | 15.5 |
| Walking one block | 3.0 | 5.0 | 6.0 | 6.6 | 6.4 |
| Walking several blocks*** | 4.0 | 9.8 | 11.7 | 11.5 | 12.0 |
| Walking more than a mile*** | 7.9 | 15.1 | 17.5 | 17.5 | 19.9 |
| **Health diagnoses (*Ever*)** | | | | | |
| Asthma** | 15.5 | 20.7 | 21.3 | 20.6 | 26.2 |
| Diabetes | 10.8 | 14.8 | 15.2 | 11.6 | 16.2 |
| High blood pressure* | 28.0 | 32.4 | 37.8 | 33.2 | 36.9 |
| Heart disease | 3.0 | 6.5 | 5.4 | 6.1 | 6.8 |
| Lung disease*** | 2.0 | 2.5 | 2.9 | 2.8 | 4.0 |
| Arthritis** | 15.2 | 23.6 | 24.7 | 24.1 | 23.9 |
| Breast cancer | 1.8 | 1.5 | 1.4 | 1.9 | 2.3 |
| Other type of cancer | 5.5 | 4.8 | 3.7 | 3.6 | 2.6 |

**Mental health diagnoses (*Ever*)**

| | | | | | |
|---|---|---|---|---|---|
| Depression** | 14.6 | 18.6 | 19.7 | 22.6 | 24.6 |
| Other mental illness | 5.1 | 8.2 | 7.3 | 8.5 | 10.1 |
| **Mental health symptomology (*Past 30 days*)** | | | | | |
| Percent with moderate depression or higher*** | 4.0 | 10.2 | 8.1 | 10.9 | 12.6 |
| Percent with PTSD | 4.3 | 7.1 | 7.0 | 6.9 | 7.38 |

Note: *$p < 0.05$, **$p < 0.01$, **=$p < 0.001$.

and feel worn out compared to residents in cold spots, and residents of cold spots were also more likely to report their health as excellent compared to residents in hot spots. Notably, nearly 76 percent of residents on cold streets indicated their health as excellent, compared to 61.1 percent in combined hot spots. While the differences in Wave 3 (Table 4) are not as strong, they are still consistent with the earlier two waves. For instance, 6.4 percent of residents in cold spots reported that they get sick more than other people, while 15 percent of residents in combined-drug-and-violent-crime hot spots reported the same perception that they get sick more than others. When combining the four items into a quality of health scale and examining the differences across the segment types, scores are consistently higher in the hot spots for all three waves (see Table 6).

### 4.2.3.2 Health Problems and Daily Activities

In addition to individuals' perception of their overall health, perhaps a more indicative measure of health is how daily activities are impacted by health problems. Survey respondents were asked if their health limits their ability to complete several different daily activities such as bathing and dressing, bending down or kneeling, carrying groceries, climbing stairs, and walking various distances. Although not every item reached statistical significance across the five types of street segments, the pattern consistently highlights that residents of hot spots are impacted to a greater extent by their health in completing daily activities. For example, in Wave 2, almost 17 percent of residents in violent, drug, and combined hot spots reported that their health impacts their ability to carry out strenuous activities and roughly 15–16 percent said that their health impacts them when climbing several flights of stairs. This can be compared to 8 percent and 5.8 percent, respectively, for residents of cold spots. It is also noteworthy that as the difficulty of the daily activity increases, such as walking one block, walking several blocks, and walking more than a mile, the differences generally become larger, where less-difficult activities have smaller differences across the segment types. Additionally, the differences across segment types also increase in a linear fashion from cold spots to combined hot spots. These patterns remain similar for the third wave of data collection as well (see Table 4). The ten items, or activities, used to measure the impact of health on daily life were also combined into a single scale for each wave, presented in Table 7. It is evident that completing daily activities is significantly more challenging for residents of crime hot spots.

### 4.2.3.3 Health Diagnoses

In regard to health diagnoses, high blood pressure is consistently higher in crime hot spots for all three waves, while there are differences in terms of which

**Table 4** Wave 3 health measures by segment type

| | Street segment type | | | | |
|---|---|---|---|---|---|
| | Cold | Cool | Drug | Violent | Combined |
| | % | % | % | % | % |
| **Overall health status*** (*Very poor/Poor*) | 4.3 | 7.7 | 7.2 | 9.7 | 9.7 |
| **Quality of health** (*Mostly true/Definitely true*) | | | | | |
| You seem to get sick more than other people** | 6.4 | 9.6 | 10.5 | 11.0 | 15.0 |
| You often feel worn out[†] | 2.7 | 3.2 | 3.5 | 3.5 | 3.6 |
| You expect your health to get worse | 16.3 | 16.6 | 14.1 | 18.0 | 16.5 |
| Your health is excellent*** | 64.7 | 58.2 | 57.5 | 51.7 | 56.6 |
| **Daily activities impacted by health** (*A lot*) | | | | | |
| Bathing or dressing yourself | 2.4 | 4.7 | 3.9 | 5.1 | 4.1 |
| Bending down or kneeling* | 6.0 | 10.8 | 10.2 | 12.7 | 10.0 |
| Doing housework[†] | 5.8 | 9.4 | 8.5 | 10.3 | 10.3 |
| Carrying groceries* | 3.1 | 7.6 | 8.4 | 8.5 | 10.1 |
| Doing strenuous activities*** | 8.4 | 15.5 | 16.2 | 18.5 | 19.0 |

**Table 4** (cont.)

| | Street segment type | | | | |
| | Cold | Cool | Drug | Violent | Combined |
| | % | % | % | % | % |
|---|---|---|---|---|---|
| Climbing one flight of stairs† | 4.5 | 8.0 | 8.0 | 9.3 | 9.5 |
| Climbing several flights of stairs*** | 6.7 | 12.7 | 16.1 | 16.7 | 15.4 |
| Walking one block† | 4.2 | 6.4 | 7.5 | 8.7 | 8.1 |
| Walking several blocks** | 5.9 | 10.9 | 12.8 | 14.0 | 13.6 |
| Walking more than a mile*** | 8.5 | 16.6 | 17.5 | 20.7 | 17.8 |
| **Health diagnoses** (*Ever*) | | | | | |
| Asthma | 18.6 | 17.8 | 20.6 | 23.3 | 21.6 |
| Diabetes* | 12.0 | 15.8 | 14.2 | 11.9 | 19.0 |
| High blood pressure* | 26.8 | 33.3 | 36.8 | 36.1 | 37.5 |
| Heart disease | 4.4 | 7.6 | 5.5 | 6.5 | 7.7 |
| Lung disease† | 2.4 | 2.2 | 2.4 | 3.5 | 4.9 |
| Arthritis | 18.6 | 23.1 | 23.1 | 24.5 | 24.2 |
| Breast cancer | 3.3 | 2.2 | 1.2 | 1.4 | 1.8 |

| | | | | | |
|---|---|---|---|---|---|
| Other type of cancer | 6.7 | 4.4 | 4.4 | 4.6 | 2.8 |
| **Mental health diagnoses** (*Ever*) | | | | | |
| Depression** | 12.4 | 17.6 | 20.1 | 22.3 | 20.1 |
| Bipolar*** | 3.0 | 6.3 | 9.8 | 10.5 | 9.2 |
| Schizophrenia* | 0.8 | 1.5 | 3.2 | 3.2 | 1.9 |
| PTSD† | 2.7 | 5.7 | 5.5 | 7.1 | 6.2 |
| Other mental illness† | 5.6 | 3.0 | 6.7 | 4.8 | 2.8 |
| **Mental health symptomology** (*Past 30 days*) | | | | | |
| Percent with moderate depression or higher** | 3.5 | 7.2 | 6.6 | 9.7 | 8.0 |
| Percent with PTSD* | 4.1 | 6.8 | 7.3 | 9.9 | 9.1 |

**Note:** †$p < 0.1$, *$p < 0.05$, **$p < 0.01$, ***$p < 0.001$.

**Table 5** Overall health status by segment type

| | | Cold (n = 46) | Cool (n = 100) | Drug (n = 120) | Violent (n = 126) | Combined (n = 55) | |
|---|---|---|---|---|---|---|---|
| | | Mean (SD) | Mean (SD) | Mean (SD) | Mean (SD) | Mean (SD) | F-score |
| | Wave 1 | 2.66 (5.67) | 5.38 (7.88) | 5.80 (8.52) | 7.30 (9.64) | 7.43 (8.11) | 3.09* |
| Time | Wave 2 | 4.57 (8.43) | 6.54 (9.01) | 6.77 (8.28) | 7.73 (11.58) | 10.33 (11.20) | 2.47* |
| | Wave 3 | 4.41 (9.13) | 7.74 (9.78) | 7.24 (11.55) | 9.74 (11.40) | 9.68 (11.28) | 2.55* |

Note: *$p < 0.05$, **$p < 0.01$, ***$p < 0.001$.

**Table 6** Quality of health scale by segment type

|  |  | Type of street segment | | | | | |
|---|---|---|---|---|---|---|---|
|  |  | **Cold**<br>($n = 46$) | **Cool**<br>($n = 100$) | **Drug**<br>($n = 120$) | **Violent**<br>($n = 126$) | **Combined**<br>($n = 55$) | |
|  |  | **Mean (SD)** | **Mean (SD)** | **Mean (SD)** | **Mean (SD)** | **Mean (SD)** | ***F*-score** |
| Time | Wave 1 | 3.19 (0.24) | 3.08 (0.21) | 3.03 (0.24) | 3.01 (0.26) | 2.98 (0.26) | 6.37*** |
|  | Wave 2 | 3.16 (0.24) | 3.02 (0.26) | 3.08 (0.22) | 3.01 (0.27) | 2.98 (0.26) | 4.62** |
|  | Wave 3 | 3.16 (0.21) | 3.03 (0.25) | 3.04 (0.23) | 2.98 (0.21) | 3.02 (0.25) | 5.50*** |

**Note:** *$p < 0.05$, **$p < 0.01$, ***$p < 0.001$.

**Table 7** Daily activities impacted by health scale by segment type

| | | | | Type of street segment | | | | | |
| --- | --- | --- | --- | --- | --- | --- | --- | --- | --- |
| | | **Cold**<br>($n = 46$) | **Cool**<br>($n = 100$) | **Drug**<br>($n = 120$) | **Violent**<br>($n = 126$) | **Combined**<br>($n = 55$) | | | |
| | | **Mean (SD)** | **Mean (SD)** | **Mean (SD)** | **Mean (SD)** | **Mean (SD)** | *F*-score |
| Time | Wave 1 | 1.14 (0.13) | 1.24 (0.19) | 1.31 (0.19) | 1.31 (0.18) | 1.38 (0.21) | 13.26*** |
| | Wave 2 | 1.15 (0.14) | 1.27 (0.20) | 1.29 (0.20) | 1.30 (0.20) | 1.32 (0.22) | 6.10*** |
| | Wave 3 | 1.18 (0.16) | 1.30 (0.26) | 1.33 (0.20) | 1.36 (0.23) | 1.35 (0.21) | 5.80*** |

Note: *$p < 0.05$, **$p < 0.01$, ***$p < 0.001$.

diagnoses are statistically significant for the three waves of data collection (see Tables 3 and 4). For instance, asthma diagnoses were significantly higher in crime hot spots in Wave 2, consistent with Wave 1 findings, but not significant in Wave 3. On the other hand, differences in diabetes diagnoses were significant in Wave 3, but not Waves 1 and 2. Regardless of significance, the percentage of residents that have health diagnoses is higher in the crime hot spots, particularly when compared to cold spots. Cancers are the only exception; they are more prevalent in the cold spots.

### 4.2.3.4 Hot Spots and Mental Health

Turning to mental health, the survey focused particularly on depression and PTSD through symptomology scales from the DSM-IV for PTSD and the PHQ-9 for depression. Weisburd and White (2019) found significantly higher rates of depression and PTSD symptomology in the crime hot spots. Furthermore, through propensity score matching and weighted negative binomial regressions, Weisburd et al. (2018) compared only the violent hot spots to cold and cool spots, and found that the relationship between violent crime and PTSD remained prominent after numerous selection factors were taken into account.

When we look at the additional waves of surveys in Tables 3 and 4, the differences in rates of PTSD and depression across the segment types remain robust, with the exception of PTSD in Wave 2, which was not significant.[15] However, when cold spots are compared to the other segment types separately, PTSD is significantly lower in cold spots. In the last wave of the survey, Weiburd et al. (2011) included additional measures of diagnosed mental health disorders, specifically bipolar disorder, schizophrenia, and PTSD. Even though the base rates at the individual level are low for these diagnoses,[16] we still see significant differences in the percentage of residents who reported having been diagnosed with bipolar or schizophrenia across the segment types. In short, health disparities across the five segment types in Baltimore are evident over the course of the project.

### 4.2.3.5 Next Steps for the Study of Hot Spots and Health

Beyond understanding the prevalence and concentration of health problems on streets within neighborhoods, the next step is to examine the causal ordering and the mechanisms through which places, particularly high-crime places, impact

---

[15] Using individual-level data, the numbers of individuals with PTSD are significantly different across the five street segment types.

[16] At the individual level, 8.6 percent of residents ($n = 270$) reported having been diagnosed with bipolar disorder, 2.5 percent ($n = 78$) reported a schizophrenia diagnosis, and 5.9 percent ($n = 184$) reported being diagnosed with PTSD.

health. Similar to neighborhood-level research, relations among neighbors and collective efficacy on the street may have implications for health at microgeographic places, perhaps even more directly impacting residents, given the narrow scope and concentration of social problems. The ability of residents to participate in community organizations and be active neighbors that provide guardianship, engaging in informal social control, may be inhibited by their health, which can have implications for crime and the health of a community more broadly. The crime hot spots in Baltimore had significantly lower levels of collective efficacy (see Weisburd et al., 2020), which may be attributed, in part, to health problems among the residents on the street, a question worth examining. Therefore, there may be a causal loop where health impacts collective efficacy, in turn impacting crime levels, that then has subsequent impacts on health. Levels of collective efficacy may have a more direct impact on residents' health as well. In qualitative interviews conducted during the project in Baltimore, one woman described an incident where her husband suffered a heart attack – "he fell down in the yard and nobody initiated to help her [by] carrying [her husband] or calling the emergency ambulance to save his life." Therefore, a lack of trust among neighbors, including neighbors not being able to ask for help from one another, perhaps even avoiding and fearing their neighbors, may have an impact on people's health and ability to get care, subsequently impacting the health of the street.

Alternatively, close social ties and cohesion may enable residents to help one another or others on the street, such as someone experiencing a mental health crisis. Rather than call the police, residents may feel more comfortable in directly intervening or using informal networks to address problems. In fact, looking at mental health calls to the police on the sample of streets in Baltimore, White and colleagues (2019) found that social cohesion and community involvement reduced the likelihood of mental health calls occurring on the street. This is consistent with other research that finds that social support and trust can protect against mental health crises (Araya et al., 2006). In another study using the data from survey respondents in the third wave of data collection, specifically those who reported mental health problems, Goldberg and colleagues (2019) found that residents with depression or PTSD had more-negative views of police legitimacy and procedural justice while also reporting greater levels of fear and concerns about safety on the street, compared to the other residents that did not self-report such symptoms of mental illness. In short, crime and disorder can impact health and mental health, but health also has important implications for the social dynamics of microgeographic places. The findings from these various studies highlight the complexity of these overlapping issues and provide opportunities for new research and policy questions to be explored.

### 4.2.4 Policing and Public Health

Perhaps the most influential policy impact of research on crime and place is hot-spots policing. Given high levels of crime concentration, the police can target these microgeographic places and have a substantial impact on crime levels (Braga & Weisburd, 2022; Braga et al., 2019; Skogan & Frydl 2004; Weisburd & Green, 1995; Weisburd & Majimundar, 2018). But this is only one outcome and does not account for the many roles of police officers, the challenges of dealing with citizens, and the interconnectedness of crime with other social problems in the places police work the most. While public health may seem out of the realm of policing, the goal of protecting citizens from harm is an essential responsibility of police, which can extend to the enforcement of public health mandates in order to reduce the harm of infectious diseases.

Historically, police powers have encompassed enforcement practices that "ensure community health standards" and the authority to "enact and enforce laws for the promotion of the general welfare" (Galva et al., 2005: 20). This is just one example that demonstrates how the worlds of policing and public health may not be as distinct as commonly perceived. More directly, interactions with the police can impact the health of residents and the places they live in, whether that is causing harm through unnecessary force or providing lifesaving practices. They can be a direct line to health services, including mental health services, particularly in the places with more crime and more health problems, as was highlighted already. Aside from physical injuries from force, the police can also have negative impacts on citizens' mental health. Research based on the aftermath of the wide use of SQFs that occurred in New York City throughout the 1990s and 2000s found that contacts with the police, particularly aggressive policing, can have negative effects on health and well-being (Das & Bruckner, 2023; Geller et al., 2014). In turn, a Campbell systematic review of SQFs found more generally that SQF initiatives have strong negative mental health outcomes for those stopped (Petersen et al., 2023; Weisburd et al., 2023a). By shifting away from aggressive police practices and better identifying the social environment of crime hot spots and the needs of the people who live there, the police can develop practices that take a more holistic approach to addressing crime and the well-being of communities.

Dong, White, and Weisburd (2020) examined theoretical mechanisms thought to mitigate the negative impact on health of living in a violent-crime hot spot. They found that perceptions of police legitimacy, along with feelings of safety and collective efficacy on the street, reduced the effect of violent crime on people's health problems. Specifically, when residents perceived median levels of police legitimacy, this mediated 40 percent of the effect of violent crime on health problems. Therefore, the police building or strength-ening relationships with the community can have positive implications for health at crime hot spots.

Recent calls for police reform have also taken a critical look at police responses to calls for service that are often unrelated to crime, particularly mental and behavioral health crises. The police are the predominant response to people experiencing a mental health crisis or living with mental illness, yet they are not traditionally trained or equipped to counsel those in mental health crisis. With the development of crisis intervention teams in the 1980s, more collaborative efforts between law enforcement and the health sector are emerging. Alternative responses aimed at reducing the role of law enforcement in mental health crises, such as co-responder teams where a police officer and a mental health professional respond to mental health crises together, are being developed and implemented in agencies across the country. Taking what we know from hot-spots policing, and the influence police legitimacy can have on people's health, along with the public's demand for alternative responses, there is an opportunity for theories of crime and place to inform public health responses that target residents living in crime hot spots. This idea was piloted in Baltimore, where White and Weisburd (2018) developed a program that sent a police officer and a licensed social worker to crime hot spots and they then attempted to connect people to services, while also building trust between residents and the police. A process evaluation and qualitative interviews high-lighted the potential of the program as several individuals contacted at the crime hot spots were able to get into treatment through the program and residents expressed the helpfulness of the team, as well as positive views of the police as a result of the program.

### 4.2.5 Conclusions

There is a strong body of theory and research around land use and opportunity factors related to crime hot spots, but the complexities of social life and the experiences of those who are impacted daily from living in or near a crime hot spot have largely been ignored. Criminology and epidemiology/health research alike predominantly focus on larger neighborhood, community-level units of analysis, so there is a general lack of theorizing and data at the microgeographic level. However, to truly understand the impact crime can have on multiple aspects of people's lives and how this can subsequently impact crime and health in the community, more attention to collecting data at a microgeographic level is needed to better inform theory and practice.

## 4.3 The Importance of Ethnography in Future Crime-and-Place Studies

Quantitative methods have been key to the development of the study of crime and place. But they do not tell the whole story as they sometimes overlook important social processes and dynamics at the micro-level. In a recent discussion about the future of crime-and-place research, John Eck made a similar observation as he reflected on practical ways that scholars can advance this area of research (Olaghere & Eck, 2023). In doing so, he gently reminded crime-and-place scholars to "leave the office" to gain a more contextualized understanding of the places they study. The findings from such research, he argues, "would be stronger and more useful if [researchers] visited the places, observed behavior, and talked to people" (Olaghere & Eck, 2023: 20). This observation becomes particularly relevant in light of recent findings from Weisburd and colleagues (2020), who discovered that collective efficacy was significantly lower among people who lived in crime hot spots than it was among those living in non-hot street segments (see Weisburd et al., 2020). This finding highlights the importance of understanding how mechanisms of social control – and, by extension, collective efficacy – operate at the microgeographic level. In discussing the implications of their findings, Weisburd and colleagues (2020: 886) write: "[O]ur data suggest that it is time to consider the social context of places." This section argues that one way this can be accomplished is by expanding the methods we currently use to study microgeographic communities.[17]

The example of collective efficacy is used in this section to further this conversation by specifying how qualitative methodologies (e.g., ethnographic observation, in-depth interviews) can advance the study of crime and place. Drawing on a sample of blocks from ethnographic research, it is argued that such methods can help us understand differences between various types of microgeographic community, while also delineating how mechanisms of informal social control (and collective efficacy) might function and operate in different ways within these small units of analysis. As discussed in Section 4.3.3, the example of collective efficacy can be expanded to other elements of social contexts at microgeographic places.

### *4.3.1 Informal Social Control, Collective Efficacy, and Microgeographic Communities*

One of the most enduring theoretical frameworks in criminology can be traced to the Chicago School, a school of thought that focused on explaining why some

---

[17] Section 4.3 was drafted by Amarat Zaatut.

communities are able to exert greater levels of informal social control than others. Emerging from this tradition is Shaw and McKay's (1942) social disorganization theory, which attempted to account for the spatial distribution and concentration of delinquency that they observed in certain areas in the city of Chicago. Central to their argument is that structural forces or neighborhood-level factors, such as poverty, residential instability, and racial and ethnic heterogeneity, are likely to undermine informal social control in communities and increase crime because residents are less likely to work together to enforce shared norms and maintain order.

Extending this notion of social disorganization, Sampson and colleagues (1997) used the term *collective efficacy* to further specify the intervening mechanisms of informal social control and account for variations in the spatial concentration of crime across different neighborhoods. Defined as "social cohesion among neighbors combined with their willingness to intervene on behalf of the common good," the concept of collective efficacy refers to the ability of neighborhood residents to control and supervise the behaviors of other local residents, especially teenagers and adolescents (Sampson et al., 1997: 918). This mechanism of self-policing within the community broadly relies on two main elements that form the foundation of collective efficacy. The first is social cohesion or trust among residents, which forms when neighbors are socially tied and connected to one another, leading to the development of shared norms and expectations about acceptable forms of behavior. In this way, social networks play a crucial role in the creation of cohesion among residents and help residents tackle common problems they face, including crime and disorder. The second component of collective efficacy is the willingness of residents to collectively intervene to control crime in their neighborhood. This aptitude for collective action stems from residents' willingness – and confidence in each other – to effectively band together to exert informal social control over unwanted behaviors in the community, whether that behavior is being caused by community members themselves or outsiders. In a case like this, collective efficacy would mediate the relationship between structural factors (e.g., poverty, residential instability, racial and ethnic heterogeneity) and neighborhood crime rates.

While community- and neighborhood-level theories of informal social control, including social disorganization, the systemic model, and collective efficacy, have traditionally been used to study the distribution of crime at the macro-level and across larger units of analysis (e.g., neighborhoods, communities, counties), some crime-and-place scholars have recently begun to consider their applicability to smaller units of analysis like street segments, street blocks, and addresses (see Groff, 2015; Weisburd et al., 2012).Whereas some crime-and-place scholars highlight the importance of considering collective efficacy in small places

(Weisburd et al., 2012), others have argued that community-and neighborhood-level explanations of informal social control cannot explain processes that occur at the street level (Braga & Clarke, 2014; Sherman et al., 1989). These scholars challenge the utility of social disorganization, and specifically collective efficacy, for explaining crime in micro-places, leading them to conclude that "it's always dangerous to extend the application of the theory (in this case, collective efficacy) beyond its intended domain (in this case, neighborhoods)" (see Braga & Clarke, 2014: 489). After all, they argue, collective efficacy is not able to explain why crime hot spots are concentrated in specific locations throughout a city or in neighborhoods with high and low rates of crime. Braga and Clarke's (2014) argument centers on two main points. The first is the idea that social disorganization and collective efficacy were founded on and draw primarily from the study of crime and delinquency in neighborhoods and "larger community units such as U.S. Census tracts and block groups," which in their view "misses much of the reality of urban crime problems that vary from street to street" (Braga & Clarke, 2014: 485). Second, they argue that the variables used to measure collective efficacy in crime-and-place scholarship (such as those used in Weisburd and colleagues' [2012] Seattle study) fail to directly capture specific mechanisms of informal social control as defined by the original concept (see Sampson et al., 1997). For example, they challenged the validity of using the percentage of active voters in street segments (as an indicator of residents' civic engagement) to measure the level of collective efficacy in micro-places. Unconvinced by the ability of community-level concepts to explain crime in micro-places, they call on crime-and-place scholars to "expand our community data collection efforts beyond what is readily available" to test these concepts at the microgeographic level, otherwise "criminologists will not meaningfully advance our understanding of urban crime problems" (Braga & Clarke, 2014: 492).

In taking on the challenge to settle this debate about whether collective efficacy theory can explain the concentration (or lack) of crime in micro-places, Weisburd and colleagues (2020) sought to expand their data collection efforts by moving beyond the "readily available data" to measure collective efficacy. They developed a survey that more directly measured variations in collective efficacy across street segments with different levels of crime in the city of Baltimore, Maryland (discussed in more detail in Section 4.2). By utilizing the questions from Sampson's original study and with specific focus on street segments, the survey measured the various components of collective efficacy, including the levels of social cohesion, trust, and cooperation between residents, as well as their likelihood of intervening to suppress crime and disorder on their street blocks. As they hypothesized, they found that collective efficacy was significantly lower among people who lived in crime hot spots than it was among those living in non-hot street segments (see Weisburd et al., 2020). These findings provide support for Weisburd and colleagues' (2012) earlier claim that street segments should be treated like small-scale communities that vary in terms of their social character, including residents' behaviors, routines, attitudes, and norms – all of which influence residents' ability to exert informal social control in small places. Importantly, these findings provide strong support for the idea that the mechanisms of collective efficacy are even more important to consider in street segments because in these social settings residents are more likely to be familiar with one another and to establish ties (weak or strong) and common goals, enhancing their willingness to intervene should unwanted behaviors arise (see Gerell, 2015; Weisburd et al., 2012).

Within this realm, what is less understood is how the social context of these microgeographic spaces allows informal social control and collective efficacy to develop and be utilized as mechanisms for controlling crime (see Groff, 2015; Weisburd et al., 2020). In this context, some scholars point to the limitations of existing datasets to study mechanisms of informal social control at the microgeographic level, as much of this data relies on measurements and variables that are better suited for studying larger geographic units (i.e., census tracts, block groups). Scholars seem to agree that there is a "need for more studies [to] collect micro-level data describing situations and methods that can examine dynamic social processes [that] are critical to achieving a better understanding of how community members control crime" (Groff, 2015: 100; also see Braga & Clarke, 2014; Olaghere & Eck, 2023).

Consistent with criminologists' calls to expand their data collection efforts to better understand the social processes and dynamics that affect crime in micro-geographic places, future crime-and-place studies should consider utilizing quali-tative approaches to collect data at these small geographic units of analysis. Specifically, using ethnographic methods to study the behaviors and attitudes of residents, local businesses, local formal social control agents (including law-enforcement officers that patrol or are familiar with high-crime places), and local organizations and institutions in and around crime hot spots can enhance our understanding and serve to contextualize the places we study.

The following sections describe how and why qualitative methodologies can be particularly useful for studying high-crime places. In doing so, we use an example from research conducted by Zaatut (see Zaatut 2016; Zaatut & Jacobsen, 2023) to demonstrate how ethnographic tools such as in-depth inter-views and ethnographic observations can help us understand differences between various types of microgeographic community, while also specifying how mechanisms of social control might function and operate in different ways within these small units of analysis.

### 4.3.2 Collective Efficacy in Action: Ethnographic Evidence from the Block

The example we identify is drawn from a three-year ethnographic research project to study one of the largest Arab ethnic enclaves located in the northeastern United States. Zaatut was specifically interested in understanding how Arab immigrants within this community navigated life in a highly disadvantaged urban context. Like many deindustrialized urban American cities, Kingston[18] had high levels of poverty, crime, and physical signs of disorder. During the fieldwork and interviews with Arab immigrants who predominantly occupied the eastern part of city, residents were asked about their neighborhood and community life, as well as their relationships with their neighbors on the blocks where they lived (see Zaatut, 2016; Zaatut & Jacobsen, 2023). Just as in Weisburd and colleagues' previously mentioned study in Baltimore, this study primarily relied on Sampson's original questions about collective efficacy (though the questions were phrased to generate conversation), in an attempt to understand the degree of social cohesion and trust among residents, not just at the larger neighborhood level but also at the smaller block level.

In-depth interviews and informal conversations with residents revealed that a particular hookah lounge located on Central Avenue was the primary source of violence and disorder in the area, especially in the Arab neighborhood where a high concentration of Arab immigrants lived. Central Avenue was a commercial and nonresidential street that ran north to south through the city and was described by participants as the heart of the Arab neighborhood. This stretch of the street, which spanned about three blocks, was occupied by many ethnic establishments including shops, bakeries, restaurants, coffee shops, and other businesses, and all were operated by Arab and Muslim immigrants in the area. A large number of residents interviewed lived in the immediate vicinity of Central Avenue and on the streets that intersect with it from east to west across this stretch of blocks. Living on the blocks adjacent to Central Avenue, many of the residents experienced and witnessed various incidents of violence and disorder that often spilled over from the hookah lounge to their streets, especially at night when customers would leave the lounge.

Engaging in in-depth interviews over a period of three years with residents allowed participants to describe how this particular hot spot persisted over time and disrupted their quality of life by contributing to an increased number of shootings and disorder in and around their street segments. When describing the atmosphere this hookah spot generated in their particular street segment, one participant noted:

---

[18] Kingston is a pseudonym for the city where the research took place to protect the anonymity of research participants and their community.

> We have those outsiders . . . coming to our neighborhood, local coffee shops, and they smoke hookah and they get drunk and they party and they're outside making noise. . . . [T]his happens all the time, especially on the weekends. We always hear them; one time there was a guy who got drunk and was running completely naked here on the streets. Bottles, trash, garbage, fights – all the effects of having a bar around are coming from [this hookah place].

These descriptions were common among residents living on the two street segments that were adjacent to the lounge, who mainly observed non-Arab customers frequenting the place at night and later "spilling out to the streets" and wreaking havoc on those who lived in the area. Instances of shootings, physical fights, public intoxication, yelling, littering, breaking bottles, and damaging property were common occurrences that residents on these two street segments described. Of particular concern to Arab residents living in these street segments was the presence of alcohol and the "bring your own bottle" policy that the hookah lounge instituted, making it the only establishment in the Arab neighborhood that permitted customers to consume alcohol.

Interviews with local law-enforcement officials revealed that the hookah lounge was indeed a hot spot, with officers recalling the many complaints and calls they received about incidents related to the establishment. When asked about crime in East Kingston, police officers described East Kingston as "crime free" compared to the rest of the city and indicated that this hookah lounge was the only problematic spot that residents complained about. Law-enforcement officials also described the lounge as a crime generator and as a place that attracts mostly local troublemakers, including drug dealers, from nearby neighborhoods.

Throughout the ethnographic fieldwork, the Arab residents of the two adjacent blocks were especially determined to solve this issue and restore the peace in their respective blocks by reversing the lounge's alcohol policy. Their physical proximity to each other and their shared cultural expectations and social norms mobilized their collective action. For example, when asked to characterize their relationships with their neighbors on their block, residents noted that "everybody knows everybody" and described themselves as "tightly knit" due to their shared language and cultural and religious norms. They trusted one another to look after each other's properties and each other's kids. They also often visited each other and were frequently observed chatting with other neighbors on their front porches. This sense of social cohesion among members of the community formed the basis of their trust in one another, which in turn facilitated their willingness to solve common problems they faced. Indeed, in their first attempt to collectively solve this problem, neighbors who lived on the block often met with one another to strategize about how to control crime and restore order on their block.

Initially, they decided that the best course of action would be to leverage social ties and networks by involving one particular local institution – the mosque – in an effort to exert parochial social order. At the mosque, neighbors would meet with community religious leaders to discuss ways they could respond to the violence and disorder in their neighborhood and respective street blocks. They would also demand action from community members, including religious leaders and other respectable members of the community, who had ties to the local police department and the mayor. Residents of these two blocks, who rallied other residents from neighboring blocks, reported that they had met with the mayor himself to complain about the lounge's policies and the implications they have for crime in their communities. By leveraging both parochial and public ties, residents were ultimately successful in closing the hookah lounge. According to informal conversations with police officers and officials from City Hall, the lounge was shut down "due to a violation for indoor smoking," which resulted in a retail license suspension for the business. The campaign to close the establishment was initiated and led by residents from the most-impacted block, which had the highest number of reported incidents. This particular block also had the highest concentration of Arab immigrant households when compared with other adjacent blocks in the Arab neighborhood.

In this case, utilizing only quantitative approaches would have missed the entire context and the stories participants provided about *how* they mobilized to combat violence and disorder that frequently took place in their respective street segments. These findings suggest that street segments are not socially and culturally disconnected from the broader neighborhood context, but instead operate within them. It also reminds us that informal social control, even on street blocks, can take many forms and occur at various levels (e.g., parochial, public). Importantly, this case study highlights the importance of considering various aspects of the systemic model of crime at the microgeographic level. The interactions and ties between residents who lived on a particular street block and their relationships to their local institutions (both formal and informal) were critical in facilitating collective efficacy and regulating crime and disorder at the street level.

### 4.3.3 Toward an Ethnography of Crime and Place: Future Directions

Ethnographic methods can be particularly useful for understanding context because they allow researchers to deeply immerse themselves in the communities they study and to gain a rich and nuanced understanding of the social, cultural, and environmental factors that shape people's lives and experiences (Miller, 2011; Zaatut & DiPietro, 2023). In the context of crime and place, applying such approaches to

examine crime hot spots in small geographic locations can help us better contextualize how street blocks or street segments might vary with regard to their social
character, including residents' behaviors, routines, attitudes, and norms – all of
which shape residents' ability and capacity to mobilize collective efficacy and
informal social control at the micro-level.

To capture the social context in which crime is concentrated, crime-and-place
scholars need to step out of their offices and start talking to people who live, work,
and frequent the crime hot spots they study, along with the street segments that
immediately surround them (Olaghere & Eck, 2023). Walking around and observing both the physical and the social environment where crimes frequently occur
(e.g., addresses, street blocks, and street segments) is the first step of ethnographic
observation. By spending time in high-crime places, researchers can observe and
document the layout of the area, including the types of buildings and their condition, the frequency and type of foot traffic (e.g., residents, visitors, businesspeople,
youths), interactions between individuals on the street, if street blocks are primarily
commercial or residential, and the type of street blocks that are in close proximity
to the actual hot spot of interest. This type of detailed information can be useful in
gaining a preliminary firsthand account of the physical and social setting where
crime occurs.

While observing the physical characteristics of crime hot spots and gaining a
general feel of places is an important first step, capturing the social settings and
the processes that unfold within these settings should immediately follow. One of
the ways this can be accomplished is through qualitative or ethnographic inter-
viewing. Even though qualitative interviews are indispensable for gathering rich
data and mapping micro-level social processes, they are significantly overlooked
and underutilized in contemporary crime-and-place research. This methodological omission can be detrimental to our understanding of the processes and
patterns that take place at the interactional and situational levels, as well as the
meanings that people attribute to them and how they may ultimately contribute to
crime and deviance in places.

Unlike the structured and closed-ended format of surveys, qualitative interviews utilize semi-structured and open-ended questions, allowing researchers to
probe participants for further detail about various aspects of social life, their
perceptions of crime and deviance in their communities, and the meanings they
attach to these events (see Martin & Jacobsen, 2023). This level of detail allows
researchers to gain a deeper understanding of the underlying attitudes and
beliefs that ultimately inform participants' actions. Thus, incorporating such
methods when studying crime in microgeographic places can be advantageous
in identifying the mechanisms that shape informal social control in various
high-crime places within specific neighborhoods. This allows criminologists to

map out exactly *how* social processes unfold over time and how mechanisms of social control operate and function in these smaller units of analysis to influence crime; such a phenomenon warrants further examination in criminological research due to its implications for crime prevention.

Indeed, qualitative studies could inform crime prevention programs, especially those that seek to strengthen informal social control in crime hot spots by involving local institutions and organizations. Recently, Weisburd and colleagues (2021a) found some evidence that hot-spots policing programs that focus on strengthening collective action among residents in hot street segments have the potential to be effective in increasing collective efficacy. However, in some micro-communities, residents might be reluctant to cooperate with the police or turn to them for help. The Kingston case, for example, shows the important role that local organizations and institutions can play in strengthening collective efficacy within communities, particularly when residents have trust in those organizations that are helping them. Using such organizations to work with residents on particular street blocks might prove more fruitful in empowering collective action in some cases. Here, qualitative research can help us better tailor our prevention programs at the microgeographic level by considering the context of places, including local residents' norms and values.

In sum, incorporating ethnographic research strategies into studies examining the relationship between crime and place can significantly advance our understanding of the processes through which places go from crime hot spots to cool spots over time, along with the possible reasons for these transformations. Collective efficacy has been used in this section as an example, but this example illustrates the potential for qualitative work to advance crime-and-place research more generally. It is time for criminologists in this area to make the scene of crime and place. This will enrich both theoretical and empirical inquiry in this area.

# References

Abraham, J., & Ceccato, V. (2022). Crime and safety in rural areas: A systematic review of the English-language literature 1980–2020. *Journal of Rural Studies, 94*, 250–273. https://doi.org/10.1016/j.jrurstud.2022.05.010.

Accordino, J., & Johnson, G. T. (2000). Addressing the vacant and abandoned property problem. *Journal of Urban Affairs, 22*(3), 301–315. https://doi.org/10.1111/0735-2166.00058.

Akers, T., Potter, R., & Hill, C. (2013). *Epidemiological Criminology: A Public Health Approach to Crime and Violence.* San Francisco, CA: Jossey-Bass/Wiley.

Ambrey, C. L., Fleming, C. M., & Manning, M. (2014). Perception or reality, what matters most when it comes to crime in your neighbourhood? *Social Indicators Research, 119*, 877–896.

America Counts. (2017). What is rural America? One in five Americans live in rural areas. US Census Bureau, August 9. www.census.gov/library/stories/2017/08/rural-america.html (accessed September 11, 2024).

Andresen, M. A. (2007). Location quotients, ambient populations, and the spatial analysis of crime in Vancouver, Canada. *Environment and Planning A: Economy and Space, 39*(10), 2423–2444. https://doi.org/10.1068/a38187.

Andresen, M. A. (2013). Measuring crime specialization using the location quotient. In *The Science of Crime Measurement: Issues for Spacially Referenced Crime Data.* Abingdon: Routledge, 71–85.

Andresen, M. A., Curman, A. S., & Linning, S. J. (2017a). The trajectories of crime at places: Understanding the patterns of disaggregated crime types. *Journal of Quantitative Criminology, 33*, 427–449.

Andresen, M. A., Linning, S. J., & Malleson, N. J. (2017b). Crime at places and spatial concentrations: Exploring the spatial stability of property crime in Vancouver BC, 2003–2013. *Journal of Quantitative Criminology, 33*, 255–275.

Andresen, M. A., Wuschke, K., Kinney, J. B., Brantingham, P. J., & Brantingham, P. L. (2009). Cartograms, crime and location quotients. *Crime Patterns and Analysis, 2*(1), 31–46. https://core.ac.uk/reader/286447480 (accessed July 14, 2023).

Ansell, C., & Gash, A. (2018). Collaborative platforms as a governance strategy. *Journal of Public Administration Research and Theory, 28*(1), 16–32.

Antunes, G. E., & Plumlee, J. P. (1977). The distribution of an urban public service: Ethnicity, socioeconomic status, and bureaucracy as determinants of the quality of neighborhood streets. *Urban Affairs Quarterly*, *12*(3), 313–332. https://doi.org/10.1177/107808747701200305.

Araya, M., Chotai, J., Komproe, I. H., & de Jong, J. T. V. M. (2006). Effect of trauma on quality of life as mediated by mental distress and moderated by coping and social support among postconflict displaced Ethiopians. *Quality of Life Research*, *16*, 915–927.

Ariel, B. (2011). Conducting low-cost experiments: A workshop. Presented at the Annual American Society of Criminology (Washington, DC), November 6.

Ariel, B. (2023a). Implementation issues with hot spot policing. *International Journal of Law, Crime and Justice*, 75, 100629.

Ariel, B. (2023b). The substitutability and complementarity of private security with public police: The case of violence against women and girls in the rail network of the United Kingdom. In E. A. Blackstone, S. Hakim, and B. Meehan (eds.), *Handbook on Public and Private Security*. Cham: Springer Nature, 193–222.

Ariel, B., Bland, M., & Sutherland, A. (2017). "Lowering the threshold of effective deterrence" – Testing the effect of private security agents in public spaces on crime: A randomized controlled trial in a mass transit system. *PLoS One*, *12*(12), e0187392.

Ariel, B., Garner, G., Strang, H., & Sherman, L. W. (2019a). Creating a critical mass for a global movement in evidence-based policing: The Cambridge Pracademia. Paper presented at the 2019 Drapkin Symposium, Hebrew University, Jerusalem, Israel.

Ariel, B., Sherman, L., & Newton, M. (2019b). Testing hot-spots police patrols against no-treatment controls: Temporal and spatial deterrence effects in the London Underground experiment. *Criminology*, *58*(1), 8:101–128.

Ariel, B., Weinborn, C., & Boyle, A. (2015). Can routinely collected ambulance data about assaults contribute to reduction in community violence? *Emergency Medicine Journal*, *32*(4), 308–313.

Ariel, B., Weinborn, C., & Sherman, L. W. (2016). "Soft" policing at hot spots – Do police community support officers work? A randomized controlled trial. *Journal of Experimental Criminology*, *12*, 277–317.

Baranyi, G., Di Marco, M. H., Russ, T. C., Dibben, C., & Pearce, J. (2021). The impact of neighbourhood crime on mental health: A systematic review and meta-analysis. *Social Science and Medicine*, 282, 114106.

Barclay, E., Donnermeyer, J. F., & Jobes, P. C. (2004). The dark side of Gemeinschaft: Criminality within rural communities. *Crime Prevention and Community Safety*, *6*(3), 7–22. https://doi.org/10.1057/palgrave.cpcs.8140191.

Bartram, R. (2019). Going easy and going after: Building inspections and the selective allocation of code violations. *City and Community*, *18*(2), 594–617.

Bauchner, H., Rivara, F. P., Bonow, R. O., Bressler, N. M., Disis, M. L., Heckers, S., Josephson, S. A., Kibbe, M. R., Piccirillo, J. F., Redberg, R. F., Rhee, J. S., & Robinson, J. K. (2017). Death by gun violence – A public health crisis. *JAMA: Journal of the American Medical Association*, *318*(18), 1763–1764. https://doi.org/10.1001/jama.2017.16446.

Bernasco, W., & Steenbeek, W. (2017). More places than crimes: Implications for evaluating the law of crime concentration at place. *Journal of Quantitative Criminology*, *33*(3), 451–467. https://doi.org/10.1007/s10940-016-9324-7.

Bichler, G. (2021). Hanging out in hyperspace: Risky places redefined. Risky Places for Crime Seminar Series 2021 (KTH Royal Institute of Technology Safeplaces Network and Nottingham Trent University Criminology Department), January 21–November 18. https://play.kth.se/media/Risky+PlacesA+Hanging+out+in+HyperspaceA+Risky+places+Redefined+by+Prof.+Gisela+Bichler/0_uusntvsq (accessed March 29, 2023).

Bichler, G., Malm, A., & Enriquez, J. (2014). Magnetic facilities: Identifying the convergence settings of juvenile delinquents. *Crime and Delinquency*, *60*(7), 971–998.

Binswanger, I. A., Stern, M. F., Deyo, R. A., Heagerty, P. J., Cheadle, A., Elmore, J. G., & Koepsell, T. D. (2007). Release from prison – A high risk of death for former inmates. *New England Journal of Medicine*, *356*, 157–165.

Birks, D., Townsley, M., & Hart, T. (2023). *Predictive Policing in an Australian Context: Assessing Viability and Utility.* Trends and Issues in Crime and Criminal Justice No. 666. Canberra: Australian Institute of Criminology. https://doi.org/10.52922/ti78870.

Bland, M., Ariel, B., & Ridgeon, N. (eds.) (2022). *The Crime Analyst's Companion.* Cham: Springer Nature.

Bloch, P. B., & Specht, D. (1973). *Neighborhood Team Policing: Prescriptive Package.* Washington, DC: US Department of Justice, Law Enforcement Assistance Administration (LEAA), and National Institute of Law Enforcement and Criminal Justice. https://files.eric.ed.gov/fulltext/ED099620.pdf (accessed September 5, 2024).

Bond, B. J., & Nader, E. (2018). Institutionalizing place-based policing. The adoption of a case of place approach. *Policing: An International Journal*, *41*(3), 372–385.

Bouffard, L. A., & Muftić, L. R. (2006). The "rural mystique": Social disorganization and violence beyond urban communities. *Western Criminology Review*, *7*(3), 56–66.

Boursnell, M., & Birch, P. (2020). Becoming a pracademic: The importance of lifelong learning as a police officer in the 21st century. In P. Birch, M. Kennedy, and E. Kruger (eds.), *Australian Policing: Critical Issues in 21st Century Police Practice*. Abingdon: Routledge, 23–37.

Bowers, K. (2014). Risky facilities: Crime radiators or crime absorbers? A comparison of internal and external levels of theft. *Journal of Quantitative Criminology, 30*(3), 389–414.

Boyle, A. A., Snelling, K., White, L., Ariel, B., & Ashelford, L. (2013). External validation of the Cardiff model of information sharing to reduce community violence: Natural experiment. *Emergency Medicine Journal, 30* (12), 1020–1023.

Boyle, J., & Jacobs, D. (1982). The intracity distribution of services: A multivariate analysis. *American Political Science Review, 76*(2), 371–379.

Braga, A. A. (2001). The effects of hot spots policing on crime. *Annals of the American Academy of Political and Social Science, 578*, 104–125.

Braga, A. A. (2008). *Problem-Oriented Policing and Crime Prevention*, 2nd ed. Boulder, CO: Lynne Rienner.

Braga, A. A. (2016). The value of "pracademics" in enhancing crime analysis in police departments. *Policing: A Journal of Policy and Practice, 10*(3), 308–314.

Braga, A. A. (2023). Gun violence, community harm, and street stops. *Policing: A Journal of Policy and Practice, 17*(3), paac009.

Braga, A. A., & Bond, B. (2008). Policing crime and disorder hot spots: A randomized controlled trial. *Criminology, 46*(3), 577–608.

Braga, A. A., & Clarke, R. V. (2014). Explaining high-risk concentrations of crime in the city: Social disorganization, crime opportunities, and important next steps. *Journal of Research in Crime and Delinquency, 51*(4), 480–498.

Braga, A. A., & Cook, P. (2023). *Policing Gun Violence: Strategic Reforms for Controlling Our Most Pressing Crime Problem*. New York: Oxford University Press.

Braga, A. A., Papachristos, A. V., & Hureau, D. (2010). The concentration and stability of gun violence at micro places in Boston, 1980–2008. *Journal of Quantitative Criminology, 26*(1), 33–53.

Braga, A. A., Papachristos, A. V., & Hureau, D. (2011). An ex post facto evaluation framework for place-based police interventions. *Evaluation Review, 35*(6), 592–626.

Braga, A. A., Turchan, B. S., Hureau, D. M., & Papachristos, A. V. (2019). Hot spots policing and crime reduction: An update of an ongoing systematic review and meta-analysis. *Journal of Experimental Criminology, 15*(3), 289–311.

Braga, A. A., & Weisburd, D. (2022). Does hot spots policing have meaningful impacts on crime? Findings from an alternative approach to estimating effect sizes from place-based program evaluations. *Journal of Quantitative Criminology, 38*(1), 1–22.

Braga, A. A., Weisburd, D., Waring, E., Mazerolle, L.G., Spelman, W., & Gajewski, F. (1999). Problem-oriented policing in violent crime places: A randomized controlled experiment. *Criminology, 37*, 541–580.

Branas, C. C., Cheney, R. A., MacDonald, J. M., Tam, V. W., Jackson, T. D., & Ten Have, T. R. (2011). A difference-in-differences analysis of health, safety, and greening vacant urban space. *American Journal of Epidemiology, 174* (11), 1296–1306.

Branas, C., South, E., Kondo, M., Hohl, B., Bourgois, P., Wiebe, D., & MacDonald, J. (2018). Citywide cluster randomized trial to restore blighted vacant land and its effects on violence, crime, and fear. *Proceedings of the National Academy of Sciences, 115*(12), 2946–2951.

Brantingham, P. J., & Brantingham, P. L. (1984). *Patterns in Crime*. New York: Macmillan.

Brantingham, P. J., & Brantingham, P. L. (1991 [1981]). *Environmental Criminology*. Prospect Heights, IL: Waveland Press.

Brantingham, P. J., Brantingham, P. L., & Andresen, M. A. (2017). The geometry of crime and crime pattern theory. In R. Wortley & M. Townsley (eds.), *Environmental Criminology and Crime Analysis*, 2nd ed. New York: Routledge, 98–115.

Brantingham, P. L., & Brantingham, P. J. (1993). Nodes, paths and edges: Considerations on the complexity of crime and the physical environment. *Journal of Environmental Psychology, 13*(1), 3–8.

Brants, H. S., & Ariel, B. (2023). Building bridges in place of barriers between school practitioners and researchers: On the role of embedded intermediaries in promoting evidence-based policy. *Evidence & Policy, 19*(1), 1–20.

Briggs, S. J., & Keimig, K. A. (2017). The impact of police deployment on racial disparities in discretionary searches. *Race and Justice, 7*(3), 256–275.

Brittain, A. (2022). A policing strategy abandoned after Breonna Taylor's death spreads to other cities. *Washington Post*, March 31. www.washingtonpost .com/investigations/interactive/2022/place-network-policing-strategy/

Browning, C. R., & Cagney, K. A. (2003). Moving beyond poverty: Neighborhood structure, social processes, and health. *Journal of Health and Social Behavior, 44*(4), 552–571. https://doi.org/10.2307/1519799.

Buerger, M. (2007). Third-party policing: Futures and evolutions. In J. A. Schafer (ed.), *Policing 2020: Exploring the Future of Crime, Communities, and Policing*. Quantico, VA: US Department of Justice,

Federal Bureau of Investigation, Futures Working Group, 452–486. https://justicestudies.com/pdf/policing2020.pdf.

Buerger, M. E., & Mazerolle, L. G. (1998). Third-party policing: A theoretical analysis of an emerging trend. *Justice Quarterly, 15*(2), 301–327.

Bursik, R. J., & Grasmick, H. G. (1993). *Neighborhoods and Crime: The Dimensions of Effective Community Control.* Lanham, MD: Lexington Books.

Byrne, J., & Marx, G. (2011). Technological innovations in crime prevention and policing: A review of the research on implementation and impact. *Journal of Police Studies, 20*(3), 17–40.

Ceccato, V., & Dolmen, L. (2011). Crime in rural Sweden. *Applied Geography, 31*(1), 119–135. https://doi.org/10.1016/j.apgeog.2010.03.002.

Ceccato, V., Ercin, E., Hazanov, J., Elfström, S., & Sampaio, A. (2023). Safety in a public library: The perspective of visitors and staff. *Library Management, 44*(3/4), 229–245. https://doi.org/10.1108/LM-12-2022-0127.

Chilenski, S. M., Syvertsen, A. K., & Greenberg, M. T. (2015). Understanding the link between social organization and crime in rural communities. *Journal of Rural and Community Development, 10*(1), 109–127. www.ncbi.nlm.nih.gov/pmc/articles/PMC4482473/ (accessed July 14, 2023).

Cingranelli, D. L. (1981). Race, politics and elites: Testing alternative models of municipal service distribution. *American Journal of Political Science, 25*(4), 664–692. https://doi.org/10.2307/2110758.

Clarke, R. V. (1980). Situational crime prevention: Theory and practice. *British Journal of Criminology, 20*(2), 136–147.

Clarke, R. V. (1983). Situational crime prevention: Its theoretical basis and practical scope. *Crime and Justice: An Annual Review of Research,* 4, 225–256.

Clarke, R. V., & Cornish, D. B. (1985). Modeling offender's decisions: A framework for research and policy. In M. Tonry and N. Morris (eds.), *Crime and Justice: An Annual Review of Research, Volume 6.* Chicago, IL: University of Chicago Press, 23–42.

Clarke, R.V., & Weisburd, D. (1994). Diffusion of crime control benefits: Observations on the reverse of displacement. *Crime Prevention Studies,* 2, 165–184.

Cohen, L. E., & Felson, M. (1979). Social change and crime rate trends: A routine activity approach. *American Sociological Review, 44*(4), 588–608.

Cohen, J., & Ludwig, J. (2002). Policing crime guns. In P. Cook and J. Ludwig (eds.), *Evaluating Gun Policy: Effects on Crime and Violence.* Washington, DC: Brookings Institution Press, 217–239.

Crossley, T. F., & Kennedy, S. (2002). The reliability of self-assessed health status. *Journal of Health Economics*, *21*(4), 643–658.

Curry, A., Latkin, C., & Davey-Rothwell, M. (2008). Pathways to depression: The impact of neighborhood violent crime on inner-city residents in Baltimore, Maryland, USA. *Social Science* and *Medicine*, *67*(1), 23–30.

Das, A., & Bruckner, T. A. (2023). New York City's stop, question, and frisk policy and psychiatric emergencies among Black Americans. *Journal of Urban Health*, *100*, 255–268. https://doi-org.libproxy.uwyo.edu/10.1007/s11524-022-00710-x.

DeHoog, R. H. (1997). Urban service delivery. In R. Vogel (ed.), *Handbook of Research on Urban Politics and Policy in the United States*. Westport, CT: Greenwood Press, 197–209.

DeKeseredy, W. S. (1990). Male peer support and woman abuse: The current state of knowledge. *Sociological Focus*, *23*(2), 129–139. www.jstor.org/stable/20831540

Deller, S. C., & Deller, M. A. (2010). Rural crime and social capital. *Growth and Change*, *41*(2), 221–275. https://doi.org/10.1111/j.1468-2257.2010.00526.x.

Demsetz, H. (1967). Toward a theory of property rights. *American Economic Review*, *57*(2), 347–359.

den Heyer, G. (2022). An examination of alternative methods for undertaking police research. In *Evidence-Based Policing: Uses, Benefits and Limitations*. Cham: Springer International, 157–171.

Desmond, M. (2017). *Evicted: Poverty and Profit in the American City*. New York: Crown.

Dickinson, J., Fowler, A., & Griffiths, T. L. (2022). Pracademics? Exploring transitions and professional identities in higher education. *Studies in Higher Education*, *47*(2), 290–304.

Diez Roux, A. V., & Mair, C. (2010). Neighborhoods and health. *Annals of the New York Academy of Science*, *1186*(1), 125–145. https://doi.org/10.1111/j.1749-6632.2009.05333.x.

Dong, B., White, C., & Weisburd, D. (2020). Poor health at violent crime hotspots: Mitigating the co-morbidity through policing. *American Journal of Preventive Medicine*, *58*(6), 799–806. https://doi.org/10.1016/j.amepre.2019.12.012.

Donnermeyer, J. F. (ed.) (2016). *The Routledge International Handbook of Rural Criminology*. London: Routledge. https://doi.org/10.4324/9781315755885.

Donnermeyer, J. F., & DeKeseredy, W. S. (2014). *Rural Criminology*, Abingdon: Routledge. www.routledge.com/Rural-Criminology/Donnermeyer-DeKeseredy/p/book/9780415634380 (accessed July 14, 2023).

Douglas, S., & Braga, A. A. (2021). Non-traditional research partnerships to aid the adoption of evidence-based policing. In E. L. Piza and B. C. Welsh (eds.), *The Globalization of Evidence-Based Policing: Innovations in Bridging the Research–Practice Divide.* Abingdon: Routledge, 178–190.

Douglas, S., & Welsh, B. C. (2022). There has to be a better way: Place managers for crime prevention in a surveillance society. *International Journal of Comparative and Applied Criminal Justice, 46*(1), 67–80.

Drover, P., & Ariel, B. (2015). Leading an experiment in police body-worn video cameras. *International Criminal Justice Review, 25*(1), 80–97.

Du Bois, W. E. B. (1973 [1899]). *The Philadelphia Negro.* Millwood, NY: Kraus-Thomson Organization.

Eck, J. E. (1995). A general model of the geography of illicit retail market-places. In J. E. Eck and D. Weisburd (eds.), *Crime and Place.* Monsey, NY: Willow Tree Press, 67–93.

Eck, J. E. (2002). Preventing crime at places. In L. W. Sherman, D. P. Farrington, B. C. Welsh, and D. L. Mackenzie (eds.), *Evidence-Based Crime Prevention.* New York: Routledge, 241–294.

Eck, J. E. (2015). There is nothing so theoretical as good practice: Police-researcher coproduction of place theory. In E. Cochbain and J. Knutsson (eds.), *Applied Police Research.* New York: Routledge, 129–140.

Eck, J. E., & Clarke, R. V. (2003). Classifying common police problems: A routine activity approach. In M. J. Smith and D. B. Cornish (eds.), *Theory for Practice in Situational Crime Prevention.* Monsey, NY: Criminal Justice Press, 7–39.

Eck, J. E., Clarke, R.V., & Guerette, R. T. (2007). Risky facilities: Crime concentration in homogeneous sets of establishments and facilities. In G. Farrell, K. J. Bowers, S. D. Johnson, and M. Townsley (eds.), *Imagination for Crime Prevention.* Monsey, NY: Criminal Justice Press, 225–264.

Eck, J. E., & Eck, E. B. (2012). Crime place and pollution: Expanding crime reduction options through a regulatory approach. *Criminology and Public Policy, 11*(2), 281–316.

Eck, J. E., & Guerette, R. T. (2012). Place-based crime prevention: Theory, evidence, and policy. In B. Welsh and D. Farrington (eds.), *The Oxford Handbook of Crime Prevention.* New York: Oxford University Press, 354–383.

Eck, J. E., Linning, S. J., & Herold, T. D. (2023). *Place Management and Crime: Ownership and Property Rights as a Source of Social Control.* SpringerBriefs in Criminology. Cham: Springer International.

Eck, J. E., Linning, S. J., & Bowers, K. (2024). Does crime in places stay in places? Evidence for crime radiation from three narrative reviews.

*Aggression and Violent Behavior, 78*, 101955. https://doi.org/10.1016/j.avb .2024.101955.

Eck, J. E., & Madensen, T. (2013). Situational crime prevention makes problem-oriented policing work: The importance of interdependent theories for effective policing. In G. Farrell and N. Tilley (eds.), *The Reasoning Criminologist: Essays in Honor of Ronald V. Clarke*. New York: Routledge, 80–92.

Eck, J. E., & Weisburd, D. (1995). Crime places in crime theory. In J. E. Eck and D. Weisburd (eds.), *Crime and Place*. Crime Prevention Studies, vol. 4. Monsey, NY: Criminal Justice Press, 1–33.

Economic Research Service. (2023). Rural poverty and well-being: Overview. US Department of Agriculture, Economic Research Service. www.ers .usda.gov/topics/rural-economy-population/rural-poverty-well-being/ (accessed September 11, 2024).

Elinson, Z. (2022). Murders in U.S. cities were near record highs in 2021. *Wall Street Journal*, January 6. www.wsj.com/articles/murders-in-u-s-cities-were-near-record-highs-in-2021-11641499978 (accessed September 9, 2024).

Evans, D. J., & Herbert, D. T. (1989). *The Geography of Crime*. London: Routledge.

Fagan, J., & Davies, G. (2000). Street stops and broken windows: Terry, race, and disorder in New York City. *Fordham Urban Law Journal, 28*(2), 457–504.

Famega, C., Hinkle, J. C., & Weisburd, D. (2017). Why getting inside the "black box" is important: Examining treatment implementation and outputs in policing experiments. *Police Quarterly, 20*(1), 106–132.

Farrington, D. P. (1995). Crime and physical health: Illnesses, injuries, accidents and offending in the Cambridge Study. *Criminal Behavior and Mental Health, 5*, 261–278.

Felson, M. (1987). Routine activities and crime prevention in the developing metropolis. *Criminology, 25*(4), 911–932.

Felson, M. (1995). Those who discourage crime. In J. E. Eck and D. Weisburd (eds.), *Crime and Place*. Monsey, NY: Willow Tree Press, 53–66.

Felson, M. (2003). The process of co-offending. In M. J. Smith and D. B. Cornish (eds.), *Theory for Practice in Situational Crime Prevention*. Monsey, NY: Criminal Justice Press, 149–167.

Gostin, J. L., Mahious, C., & Looney, P. (2005). Public health strategy and the police powers of the state. *Public Health Reports, 120*(1_suppl), 20–27. https://doi.org/10.1177/00333549051200S106.

Garvin, E., Branas, C., Keddem, S., Sellman, J., & Cannuscio, C. (2013). More than just an eyesore: Local insights and solutions on vacant land and urban health. *Journal of Urban Health, 90*(3), 412–426. https://doi.org/10.1007/s11524-012-9782-7.

Geller, A., Fagan, J., Tyler, T., & Link, B. G. (2014). Aggressive policing and the mental health of young urban men. *American Journal of Public Health, 104*(12), 2321–2327. https://doi.org/10.2105/AJPH.2014.302046.

Gelman, A., Fagan, J., & Kiss, A. (2007). An analysis of New York City Police Department's "stop-and-frisk" policy in the context of claims of racial bias. *Journal of the American Statistical Association, 102*(479), 813–823.

Gentry, D., Scott, S., Meglen, J., Gill, C., Vitter, Z., Sizemore, J., & Simpson, D. (2018). *Berea CBCR Site: Final Report Summary.* Berea, KY: Partners for Education at Berea College.

Gerell, M. (2015). Collective efficacy, neighborhood and geographical units of analysis: Findings from a case study of Swedish residential neighborhoods. *European Journal on Criminal Policy and Research, 21*(3), 385–406.

Gianfredi, V., Buffoli, M., Rebecchi, A., Croci, R., Oradini-Alacreu, A., Stirparo, G., Marino, A., Odone, A., Capolongo, S., & Signorelli, C. (2021). Association between urban greenspace and health: A systematic review of literature. *International Journal of Environmental Research and Public Health, 18*(10), 5137.

Gilderbloom, J. I. (1989). Socioeconomic influences on rentals for us urban housing: Assumptions of open access to a perfectly competitive "free market" are confronted with the facts. *American Journal of Economics and Sociology, 48*(3), 273–292.

Gill, C., Vitter, Z., & Weisburd, D. (2015). *Identifying Hot Spots of Juvenile Offending: A Guide for Crime Analysts.* Washington, DC: US Department of Justice, Office of Community Oriented Policing Services. https://cops.usdoj.gov/RIC/ric.php?page=detail&id=COPS-P298.

Gill, C., Vitter, Z., & Weisburd, D. (2016). *Rainier Beach: A Beautiful Safe Place for Youth. Final Evaluation Report.* Fairfax, VA: Center for Evidence-Based Crime Policy, Department of Criminology, Law and Society, George Mason University. www.rb-safeplaceforyouth.com/wp-content/uploads/2018/03/2016-GMU-ABSPY-evaluation-report.pdf (accessed Spetember 11, 2024).

Gill, C., Wooditch, A., & Weisburd, D. (2017). Testing the "law of crime concentration at place" in a suburban setting: Implications for research and practice. *Journal of Quantitative Criminology, 33*(3), 519–545. https://doi.org/10.1007/s10940-016-9304-y.

Gladwell, M. (2019). *Talking to Strangers: What We Should Know About the People We Don't Know.* New York: Little Brown and Company.

Glaeser, E. L. (2013). Urban public finance. In A. J. Auerbach, R. Chetty, M. Feldstein, and E. Saez (eds.), *Handbook of Public Economics: Volume 5*. Amsterdam: Elsevier, 195–256.

Goldberg, V., White, C., & Weisburd, D. (2019). Perspectives of people with mental health problems at hot spots: Attitudes and perceptions of safety, crime, and the police. *Behavioral Sciences and the Law, 37*(6), 650–664.

Goldstein, H. (1990). *Problem-Oriented Policing*. Philadelphia, PA: Temple University Press.

Gómez, J. E., Johnson, B. A., Selva, M., & Sallis, J. F. (2004). Violent crime and outdoor physical activity among inner-city youth. *Preventive Medicine, 39* (5), 876–881.

Greene, J. A. (1999). Zero tolerance: A case study of police policies and practices in New York City. *Crime and Delinquency, 45*(2), 171–187.

Greene, J. R. (2014). New directions in policing: Balancing prediction and meaning in police research. *Justice Quarterly, 31*(2), 193–228.

Groff, E. (2011). Exploring "near": Characterizing the spatial extent of drinking place influence on crime. *Australian and New Zealand Journal of Criminology, 44*(2), 156–179. https://doi.org/10.1177/0004865811405253.

Groff, E. R. (2015). Informal social control and crime events. *Journal of Contemporary Criminal Justice, 31*(1), 90–106.

Groff, E. R., Ratcliffe, J. H., Haberman, C. P., Sorg, E. T., Joyce, N., & Taylor, R. B. (2015). Does what police do at hot spots matter? The Philadelphia Policing Tactics Experiment. *Criminology, 53*(1), 23–53.

Hammer, M. (2011). Crime places of comfort. Unpublished paper. University of Cincinnati.

Hammer, M. G. (2020). Place-based investigations of violent offender territories (PIVOT): An exploration and evaluation of a place network disruption violence reduction strategy in Cincinnati, Ohio. Unpublished PhD dissertation, University of Cincinnati.

Hammer, M., Christenson, B., & Madensen, T. D. (2017). P.I.V.O.T. Place-based investigations of violent offender territories: Herman Goldstein Award submission. *27th Annual Problem-Oriented Policing Conference*, Houston, TX.

Han, H. S., & Helm, S. (2023). Does demolition lead to a reduction nearby in crime associated with abandoned properties? *Housing Policy Debate, 33*(2), 331–357.

Harinam, V., Bavcevic, Z., & Ariel, B. (2022). Spatial distribution and developmental trajectories of crime versus crime severity: Do not abandon the count-based model just yet. *Crime Science, 11*, article 14. https://doi.org/10.1186/s40163-022-00176-x.

Hero, R. E. J. P. (1986). The urban service delivery literature: Some questions & considerations. *Polity, 18*(4), 659–677.

Herold, T., Engel, R., Corsaro, N., & Clouse, S. (2020). *Place Network Investigations in Las Vegas, Nevada: Program Review and Process Evaluation.* Cincinnati, OH: International Association of Chiefs of Police (IACP)/ University of Cincinnati Center for Police Research and Policy.

Hibdon, J. (2011). What's Hot and What's Not: The Effects of Individual Factors on the Identification of Hot and Cool Crime Spots. Doctoral dissertation. Fairfax, VA: George Mason University. https://hdl.handle.net/1920/6598.

Ho, H., Gilmour, J., Mazerolle, L., & Ko, R. (2023). Utilizing cyberplace managers to prevent and control cybercrimes: A vignette experimental study. *Security Journal*, March. https://doi.org/10.1057/s41284-023-00371-8.

Honoré, A. M. (1961). Ownership. In A. G. Guest (ed.), *Oxford Essays in Jurisprudence*. New York: Oxford University Press, 370–375.

Hud Exchange. (n.d.). Promise Zones overview. www.hudexchange.info/programs/promise-zones/promise-zones-overview/ (accessed September 11, 2024).

Huey, L., & Mitchell, R. J. (2016). Unearthing hidden keys: Why pracademics are an invaluable (if underutilized) resource in policing research. *Policing: A Journal of Policy and Practice, 10*(3), 300–307.

Hunter, M. A. (2013). *Black Citymakers: How the Philadelphia Negro Changed Urban America*. New York: Oxford University Press.

Jackson, M. (2010). Murder concentration and distribution patterns in London: An exploratory analysis of ten years of data. MSt paper, University of Cambridge. www.crim.cam.ac.uk/system/files/documents/jackson-m.pdf (accessed September 11, 2024).

Jacobs, J. (1956). The missing link in city redevelopment. *Architectural Forum*, June, 132–133.

Jacobs, J. (1961). *The Death and Life of Great American Cities*. New York: Vintage.

Jacques, S., & Moeller, K. (2023). Toleration by victimized coffeeshops in Amsterdam. *Crime and Delinquency, 69*(3), 510–532.

Jobes, P. C., Barclay, E., Weinand, H., & Donnermeyer, J. F. (2004). A structural analysis of social disorganisation and crime in rural communities in Australia. *Australian and New Zealand Journal of Criminology, 37*(1), 114–140. https://doi.org/10.1375/acri.37.1.114.

Johnston, D. W., Propper, C., & Shields, M. A. (2009). Comparing subjective and objective measures of health: Evidence from hypertension for the income/health gradient. *Journal of Health Economics, 28*(3), 540–552.

Jones, B. D. (1977). Distributional considerations in models of government service provision. *Urban Affairs Quarterly, 12*(3), 291–312.

Jones, B. D., & Kaufman, C. (1974). The distribution of urban public services: A preliminary model. *Administration and Society, 6*(3), 337–360.

Jones, B. D., Greenberg, S. R., Kaufman, C., & Drew, J. (1978). Service delivery rules and the distribution of local government services: Three Detroit bureaucracies. *Journal of Politics, 40*(2), 332–368.

Jones, R. W., & Pridemore, W. A. (2019). Toward an integrated multilevel theory of crime at place: Routine activities, social disorganization, and the law of crime concentration. *Journal of Quantitative Criminology, 35*(3), 543–572. https://doi.org/10.1007/s10940-018-9397-6.

Kanewske, L. C. (2023). "Things have changed around here": Perceptions of crime and safety in rural Southeastern Kentucky. Unpublished doctoral dissertation, George Mason University.

Kaylen, M., & Pridemore, W. (2012). Systematically addressing inconsistencies in the rural social disorganization and crime literature. *International Journal of Rural Criminology, 1*, 134–152. https://doi.org/10.18061/1811/53701.

Kaylen, M. T., & Pridemore, W. A. (2013). Social disorganization and crime in rural communities: The first direct test of the systemic model. *British Journal of Criminology, 53*(5), 905–923. www.jstor.org/stable/23639796.

Kelling, G., Pate, T., Dieckman, D., & Brown, C. (1974). *The Kansas City Preventive Patrol Experiment: A Technical Report*. Washington, DC: Police Foundation.

Kerner Commission. (1968). *National Advisory Commission on Civil Disorder*. Washington, DC: Government Printing Office.

Keyes, K. M., Cerdá, M., Brady, J. E., Havens, J. R., & Galea, S. (2014). Understanding the rural–urban differences in nonmedical prescription opioid use and abuse in the United States. *American Journal of Public Health, 104* (2), e52–e59. https://doi.org/10.2105/AJPH.2013.301709.

Kochel, T. (2011). Constructing hot spots policing: Unexamined consequences for disadvantaged populations and for police legitimacy. *Criminal Justice Policy Review, 22*(3), 350–374.

Kochel, T., & Weisburd, D. (2019). The impact of hot spots policing on collective efficacy: Findings from a randomized field trial. *Justice Quarterly, 36*(5), 900–928.

Kondo, M. C., Keene, D., Hohl, B. C., MacDonald, J. M., & Branas, C. C. (2015). A difference-in-differences study of the effects of a new abandoned building remediation strategy on safety. *PLoS One, 10*(7), e0129382. https://doi.org/10.1371/journal.pone.0129582.

Koper, C. S. (1995). Just enough police presence: Reducing crime and disorderly behavior by optimizing patrol time in crime hot spots. *Justice Quarterly, 12*(4), 649–672.

Koziarski, J. (2021). Examining the spatial concentration of mental health calls for police service in a small city. *Policing: A Journal of Policy and Practice, 15*(2), 1011–1028. https://doi.org/10.1093/police/paaa093.

Koziarski, J. (2023). The spatial (in)stability of mental health calls for police service. *Criminology and Public Policy, 22*(2), 293–322. https://doi.org/10.1111/1745-9133.12612.

Kuchar, L. E. (2020). Receptivity of police practitioners to pracademics. Unpublished doctoral dissertation, The William Paterson University of New Jersey.

Kuen, K., Weisburd, D., White, C., & Hinkle, J. C. (2022). Examining impacts of street characteristics on residents' fear of crime: Evidence from a longitudinal study of crime hot spots. *Journal of Criminal Justice, 82*, 101984.

Kuhns, J. B., Maguire, E. R., & Cox, S. M. (2007). Public-safety concerns among law enforcement agencies in suburban and rural America. *Police Quarterly, 10*(4), 429–454. https://doi.org/10.1177/1098611106289405.

Lam, A. (2021). Organizational misfits as creative agents of change: The case of pracademics. In E. Schuessler, P. Cohendet, and S. Svejenova (eds.), *Organizing Creativity in the Innovation Journey*. Research in the Sociology of Organizations, vol. 75. Bingley: Emerald, 163–186.

Lasswell, H. D. (1936). *Politics: Who Gets What, When, How*. New York: Whittlesey House.

Lee, M. R., & Thomas, S. A. (2010). Civic community, population change, and violent crime in rural communities. *Journal of Research in Crime and Delinquency, 47*(1), 118–147. https://doi.org/10.1177/0022427809348907.

Lee, Y. J., & Eck, J. E. (2019). Comparing measures of the concentration of crime at places. *Crime Prevention and Community Safety, 21*(4), 269–294.

Lee, Y., Eck, J. E., O, S., & Martinez, N. N. (2017). How concentrated is crime at places? A systematic review from 1970 to 2015. *Crime Science, 6*, article 6. https://doi.org/10.1186/s40163-017-0069-x.

Lee, Y., O, S., & Eck, J. E. (2022), Why your bar has crime but not mine: Resolving the land use and crime – risky facility conflict. *Justice Quarterly, 39*(5), 1009–1035.

Levander, S. (2022). Police pracademics: The merge of tacit and scientific knowledge in an old profession/young science. *Nordisk Tidsskrift for Kriminalvidenskab, 110*(1), 69–74.

Levy, F., Meltsner, A. J., & Wildavsky, A. B. (1975). *Urban Outcomes: Schools, Streets, and Libraries*. Berkeley: University of California Press.

Lieb, E. (2018). "Baltimore does not condone profiteering in squalor": The Baltimore Plan and the problem of housing-code enforcement in an American city. *Planning Perspectives, 33*(1), 75–95.

Lineberry, R. L. (1977). *Equality and Urban Policy: The Distribution of Municipal Public Services.* Beverly Hills, CA: Sage.

Lineberry, R. L., & Welch, R. E. (1974). Who gets what: Measuring the distribution of urban public services. *Social Science Quarterly, 4*(54), 700–712.

Linning, S. J., & Eck, J. E. (2021). *Whose "Eyes on the Street" Control Crime?* New York: Cambridge University Press.

Linning, S. J., & Eck, J. E. (2023). Race-based real estate practices and spuriousness in community criminology: Was the Chicago School part of a self-fulfilling prophecy? *Criminal Justice Review.* https://doi.org/10.1177/07340168231175444.

Linning, S. J., Eck, J. E., & Bowers, K. (2024). "Crime radiation theory: The co-production of crime patterns through opportunity creation and exploitation. *Crime Science.*

Linning, S. J., Olaghere, A., & Eck, J. E. (2022). Say NOPE to social disorganization criminology: The importance of creators in neighborhood social control. *Crime Science, 11*(1), article 5. https://doi.org/10.1186/s40163-022-00167-y.

Lopez, G. (2023). Policing the wrong way. *New York Times*, February 1. www.nytimes.com/2023/02/01/briefing/memphis-scorpion-unit-tyre-nichols-death.html (accessed September 11, 2024).

Lorenc, T., Clayton, S., Neary, D., Whitehead, M., Petticrew, M., Thomson, H., Cummins, S., Sowden, A., & Renton, A. (2012). Crime, fear of crime, environment, and mental health and wellbeing: mapping review of theories and causal pathways. *Health and Place, 18*(4), 757–765.

LSE Library. (2016). Charles Booth's London: Poverty maps and police notebooks. London School of Economics and Political Science. https://booth.lse.ac.uk/ (accessed October 5, 2022).

Macbeth, E., & Ariel, B. (2019). Place-based statistical versus clinical predictions of crime hot spots and harm locations in Northern Ireland. *Justice Quarterly, 36*(1), 93–126.

MacDonald, J. (2015). Community design and crime: The impact of housing and the built environment. *Crime and Justice: A Review of Research, 44*(1), 333–383.

MacDonald, J., Fagan, J., & Geller, A. (2016). The effects of local police surges on crime and arrests in New York City. *PLoS One, 11*(6), e0157223.

Madensen, T. D., & Eck, J. E. (2008). Violence in bars: Exploring the impact of place manager decision-making. *Crime Prevention and Community Safety: An International Journal, 10*(2), 111–125.

Madensen, T. D., & Eck, J. E. (2013). Crime places and place management. In F. T. Cullen and P. Wilcox (eds.), *The Oxford Handbook of Criminological Theory*. New York: Oxford University Press, 554–578.

Madensen, T., Herold, M., Hammer, M., & Christenson, B. (2017). Place-based investigations to disrupt crime place networks. *Police Chief Magazine*, April, 14–15. www.policechiefmagazine.org/research-brief-place-based-investiga tions/ (accessed September 11, 2024).

Magnusson, M. M. (2020). Bridging the gaps by including the police officer perspective? A study of the design and implementation of an RCT in police practice and the impact of pracademic knowledge. *Policing: A Journal of Policy and Practice, 14*(2), 438–455.

Maple, J. (1999). *The Crime Fighter: How You Can Make Your Community Crime Free*. New York: Broadway.

Mawby, R. I. (2007). Crime, place and explaining rural hotspots. *International Journal of Rural Crime, 1*, 21–43.

McDonald, N. C. (2008). The effect of objectively measured crime on walking in minority adults. *American Journal of Health Promotion, 22*, 433–436.

McGarrell, E., Chermak, S., Weiss, A., & Wilson, J. (2001). Reducing firearms violence through directed police patrol. *Criminology and Public Policy, 1*(1), 119–148.

McLafferty, S. L. (1984). Constraints on distributional equity in the location of public services. *Political Geography Quarterly, 3*(1), 33–47.

McLafferty, S. L., & Ghosh, A. (1982). Issues in measuring differential access to public services. *Urban Studies, 19*(4), 383–389. https://doi.org/10.1080/0042098822008061 1.

Meglen, J., & Gill, C. (2020). "Harmony in the hills": Peaks and valleys in the Berea, KY rural BCJI program. In R. J. Stokes and C. Gill (eds.), *Innovations in Community-Based Crime Prevention: Case Studies and Lessons Learned*. Cham: Springer.

Messner, S. F., Anselin, L., Baller, R. D., Hawkins, D. F., Deane, G., & Tolnay, S. E. (1999). The spatial patterning of county homicide rates: An application of exploratory spatial data analysis. *Journal of Quantitative Criminology, 15*(4), 423–450. https://doi.org/10.1023/A:1007544208712.

Meyer, O. L., Castro-Schilo, L., & Anguilar-Gaxiola, S. (2014). Determinants of mental health and self-rated health: A model of socioeconomic status, neighborhood safety, and physical activity. *American Journal of Public Health, 104*(9), 1734–1741.

Mladenka, K. R. (1989). The distribution of an urban public service: The changing role of race and politics. *Urban Affairs Quarterly, 24*(4), 556–583.

Mladenka, K. R., & Hill, K. Q. (1977). The distribution of benefits in an urban environment: Parks and libraries in Houston. *Urban Affairs Quarterly, 13*(1), 73–94.

Miller, J. (2011). Grounding the analysis of gender and crime: Accomplishing and interpreting qualitative interview research. In D. Gadd, S. Karstedt, and S. F. Messner (eds.), *The SAGE Handbook of Criminological Research Methods*. London: Sage, 49–62.

Moyer, R., MacDonald, J. M., Ridgeway, G., & Branas, C. C. (2019). Effect of remediating blighted vacant land on shootings: A citywide cluster randomized trial. *American Journal of Public Health, 109*(1), 140–144. https://doi .org/10.2105/AJPH.2018.304752.

Nivola, P. S. (1978). Distributing a municipal service: A case study of housing inspection. *Journal of Politics, 40*(1), 59–81. https://doi.org/10.2307/ 2129976.

Norton, S., Ariel, B., Weinborn, C., & O'Dwyer, E. (2018). Spatiotemporal patterns and distributions of harm within street segments: The story of the "harmspot." *Policing: An International Journal, 41*(3), 352–371.

O'Campo, P., Wheaton, B., Nisenbaum, R., Glazier, R. H., Dunn, J. R., & Chambers, C. (2015). The Neighbourhood Effects on Health and Well-being (NEHW) study. *Health and Place, 31*, 65–74.

Olaghere, A., & Eck, J. E. (2023). Crime, place and race: A dialogue furthering a race aware program of useful research. In E. Groff and C. Haberman (eds.), Understanding Crime and Place: A Methods Handbook. Philadelphia, PA: Temple University Press, 13–26.

Oxford English Dictionary. (2010). Epidemiology. In *Oxford Dictionary of English*, 3rd ed. Oxford: Oxford University Press.

Pareto, V. (1909). *Manuel d'économie politique*. Oeuvres complètes, vol. 7. Geneva: Droz.

Payne, T., & Eck, J. E. (2007) Who Owns Crime? Annual Meeting of the American Society of Criminology, Atlanta, GA, November 14–17.

Payne, T., Gallagher, K., Eck, J. E., & Frank, J. (2013). Problem framing in problem solving: A case study. *Policing: An International Journal of Police Strategies and Management, 36*(4), 670–682.

Petersen, K., Weisburd, D., Fay, S., Eggins, E., & Mazerolle, L. (2023). Police stops to reduce crime: A systematic review and meta-analysis. *Campbell Systematic Review, 19*(1), e1302.

Phelan, J. C., Link, B. G., Diez-Roux, A., Kawachi, I., & Levin, B. (2004). "Fundamental causes" of social inequalities in mortality: A test of the theory. *Journal of Health and Social Behavior, 45*(3), 265–285.

Pierce, G., Spaar, S., & Briggs, L. R. (1988). *The character of police work: Strategic and tactical implications*. Boston, MA: Center for Applied Social Research, Northeastern University.

Piza, E. L., & Feng, S. Q. (2017). The current and potential role of crime analysts in evaluations of police interventions: Results from a survey of the International Association of Crime Analysts. *Police Quarterly, 20*(4), 339–366.

Piza, E. L., Szkola, J., & Blount-Hill, K. L. (2021). How can embedded criminologists, police pracademics, and crime analysts help increase police-led program evaluations? A survey of authors cited in the evidence-based policing matrix. *Policing: A Journal of Policy and Practice, 15*(2), 1217–1231.

Piza, E. L., & Welsh, B. C. (2022). Evidence-based policing is here to stay: Innovative research, meaningful practice, and global reach. *Cambridge Journal of Evidence-Based Policing, 6*(1–2), 42–53.

Police Executive Research Forum. (2008). *Violent Crime in America: What We Know About Hot Spots Enforcement*. Washington, DC: Police Executive Research Forum.

Posner, P. L. (2009). The pracademic: An agenda for re-engaging practitioners and academics. *Public Budgeting and Finance, 29*(1), 12–26.

Potter, R. H., & Akers, T. A. (2010). Improving the health of minority communities through probation-public health collaborations: An application of the epidemiological criminology framework. *Journal of Offender Rehabilitation, 49*(8), 595–609.

Ratcliffe, J. H. (2005). Detecting spatial movement of intra-region crime patterns over time. *Journal of Quantitative Criminology, 21*(1), 103–123.

Ratcliffe, M., Burd, C., Holder, K., & Fields, A. (2016). *Defining Rural at the U.S. Census Bureau*. American Community Survey and Geography Brief No. ACSGEO-1. Washington, DC: US Census Bureau. www.census.gov/content/dam/Census/library/publications/2016/acs/acsgeo-1.pdf (accessed September 11, 2024).

Reaves, B. (2010). *Local Police Departments, 2007*. Washington, DC: US Bureau of Justice Statistics.

Reppetto, T. (1976). Crime prevention and the displacement phenomenon. *Crime and Delinquency, 22*, 166–177

Reyns, B. W. (2010). A situational crime prevention approach to cyberstalking victimization: Preventive tactics for internet users and online place managers. *Crime Prevention and Community Safety, 12*(2), 99–118.

Reyns, B. W., Henson, B., & Fisher, B. S. (2011). Being pursued online: Applying cyber lifestyle-routine activities theory to cyberstalking victimization. *Criminal Justice and Behavior, 38*(11), 1149–1169.

Rich, R. C. (1979). Neglected issues in the study of urban service distributions: A research agenda. *Urban Studies*, *16*(2), 143–156.

Roncek, D. W. (1981). Dangerous places: Crime and residential environments. *Social Forces*, *60*(1), 74–96.

Rosen, D. L., Schoenbach, V. J., & Wohl, D. A. (2008). All-cause and cause-specific mortality among men released from state prison, 1980–2005. *American Journal of Public Health*, *98*, 2278–2284.

Rosenbaum, D. (2019). The limits of hot spots policing. In D. Weisburd and A. Braga (eds.), *Police Innovation: Contrasting perspectives*, 2nd ed. New York: Cambridge University Press.

Rosenfeld, R., Deckard, M., & Blackburn, E. (2014). Effects of directed patrol and self-initiated enforcement on firearm violence: A randomized controlled study of hot spot policing. *Criminology*, *52*(3), 428–449.

Ross, C. E., & Britt, C. (1995). *Survey of Community,Crime, and Health*. Austin: University of Texas at Austin Department of Sociology and Population Research Center.

Sampson, R. J. (1990). The impact of housing policies on community social disorganization and crime. *Bulletin of the New York Academy of Medicine*, *66*(5), 526–533. https://pubmed.ncbi.nlm.nih.gov/2257384 (accessed September 11, 2024).

Sampson, R., Eck, J. E., & Dunham, J. (2010). Super controllers and crime prevention: A routine activity explanation of crime prevention success and failure. *Security Journal*, *23*(1), 37–51.

Sampson, R. J., Raudenbush, S. W., & Earls, F. (1997). Neighborhoods and violent crime: A multilevel study of collective efficacy. *Science*, *277*(5328), 918–924. https://doi.org/10.1126/science.277.5328.918.

Schaefer, A., Mattingly, M. J., & Johnson, K. M. (2016). *Child Poverty Higher and More Persistent in Rural America*. Durham: University of New Hampshire, Carsey School of Public Policy.

Shaw, C. R., & McKay, H. D. (1942). *Juvenile Delinquency and Urban Areas: A Study of Rates of Delinquents in Relation to Differential Characteristics of Local Communities in American Cities*. Chicago, IL: University of Chicago Press.

Shaw, J. (1995). Community policing against guns: Public opinion of the Kansas City gun experiment. *Justice Quarterly*, *12*(4), 695–710.

Shepard, J., Farrington, D., & Potts, J. (2004). Impact of antisocial lifestyle on health. *Journal of Public Health*, *26*(4), 347–352.

Sherman, L. W. (2021). The Cambridge Police Executive Programme: A global reach for pracademics. In E. L. Piza and B. C. Welsh (eds.), *The*

*Globalization of Evidence-Based Policing: Innovations in Bridging the Research–Practice Divide.* Abingdon: Routledge, 295–317.

Sherman, L. W., Gartin, P., & Buerger, M. E. (1989). Hot spots of predatory crime: Routine activities and the criminology of place. *Criminology, 27,* 27–55.

Sherman, L. W., Milton, C., Kelly, T. V., & MacBride, T. F. (1973). *Team Policing: Seven Case Studies.* Washington, DC: Police Foundation.

Sherman, L., & Rogan, D. (1995). Effects of gun seizures on gun violence: "Hot spots" patrol in Kansas City. *Justice Quarterly, 12,* 673–694.

Sherman, L., & Weisburd, D. (1995). General deterrent effects of police patrol in crime hot spots: A randomized controlled trial. *Justice Quarterly, 12,* 625–648.

Simon, H. A., & Bonini, C. P. (1958). The size distribution of business firms. *American Economic Review, 48*(4), 607–617.

Skogan, W., & Frydl, K. (eds.) (2004). *Fairness and Effectiveness in Policing: The Evidence. Committee to Review Research on Police Policy and Practices.* Washington, DC: National Academies Press.

Smith, D. M. (1974). Who gets what where, and how: A welfare focus for human geography. *Geography, 59*(4), 289–297.

South, E. C., Hohl, B. C., Kondo, M. C., MacDonald, J. M., & Branas, C. C. (2018). Effect of greening vacant land on mental health of community-dwelling adults: A cluster randomized trial. *JAMA (Journal of the American Medical Association) Network Open, 1*(3), e180298. https://doi.org/10.1001/jamanetworkopen.2018.0298.

South, E. C., Kondo, M. C., Cheney, R. A., & Branas, C. C. (2015). Neighborhood blight, stress, and health: A walking trial of urban greening and ambulatory heart rate. *American Journal of Public Health, 105*(5), 909–913. https://doi.org/10.2105/AJPH.2014.302526.

South, E. C., MacDonald, J., & Reina, V. (2021). Association between structural housing repairs for low-income homeowners and neighborhood crime. *JAMA (Journal of the American Medical Association) Network Open, 4*(7), e2117067. https://doi.org/10.1001/jamanetworkopen.2021.17067.

Stacy, C. P. (2018). The effect of vacant building demolitions on crime under depopulation. *Journal of Regional Science, 58*(1), 100–115. https://doi.org/10.1111/jors.12350.

Strang, H., Sherman, L., Ariel, B., Chilton, S., Braddock, R., Rowlinson, T., Cornelius, N., Jarman, R., & Weinborn, C. (2017). Reducing the harm of intimate partner violence: Randomized controlled trial of the Hampshire Constabulary CARA Experiment. *Cambridge Journal of Evidence-Based Policing, 1,* 160–173. https://doi.org/10.1007/s41887-017-0007-x.

Talen, E., & Anselin, L. (1998). Assessing spatial equity: An evaluation of measures of accessibility to public playgrounds. *Environment and Planning A, 30*(4), 595–613.

Taylor, R. B. (1997). Social order and disorder of street blocks and neighborhoods: Ecology, microecology, and the systemic model of social disorganization. *Journal of Research in Crime and Delinquency, 34*(1), 113–155. https://doi.org/10.1177/0022427897034001006.

Taylor, R. B., & Gottfredson, S. (1986). Environmental design, crime, and prevention: An examination of community dynamics. *Crime and Justice: A Review of Research, 8*, 387–416.

Telep, C. W., Mitchell, R. J., & Weisburd, D. (2014). How much time should the police spend at crime hot spots? Answers from a police agency directed randomized field trial in Sacramento, California. *Justice Quarterly, 31*, 905–933.

Tillyer, M. S., Acolin, A., & Walter, R. J. (2023). Place-based improvements for public safety: Private investment, public code enforcement, and changes in crime at microplaces across six U.S. cities. *Justice Quarterly, 40*(5), 694–724.

Tillyer, M. S., & Walter, R. J. (2019). Busy businesses and busy contexts: The distribution and sources of crime at commercial properties. *Journal of Research in Crime and Delinquency, 56*(6), 816–850. https://doi.org/10.1177/0022427819848083.

Townsley, M., Homel, R., & Chaseling, J. (2000). Repeat burglary victimisation: Spatial and temporal patterns. *Australian and New Zealand Journal of Criminology, 33*(1), 37–63. https://doi.org/10.1177/000486580003300104.

Tso, G. (2016). Police brutality is not invisible. *The Hill*, January 14. http://thehill.com/blogs/congress-blog/civil-rights/265795-police-brutality-is-not-invisible (accessed September 11, 2024).

Tyler, T. R. (2003). Procedural justice, legitimacy, and the effective rule of law. In M. Tonry (ed.), *Crime and Justice: A Review of Research, Volume 30*. Chicago, IL: University of Chicago Press, 283–357.

US Department of Health and Human Services. (2008). *National Survey on Drug Use and Health* Washington, DC: US Department of Health and Human Services.

Wain, N., & Ariel, B. (2014). Tracking of police patrol. *Policing: A Journal of Policy and Practice, 8*(3), 274–283.

Waldron, J. (1988). *The Right to Property*. New York. Oxford University Press.

Wallman, J., & Blumstein, A. (2006). After the crime drop. In A. Blumstein and J. Wallman (eds.), *The Crime Drop in America*, 2nd rev. ed. New York: Cambridge University Press, 319–348.

Weinborn, C., Ariel, B., Sherman, L. W., & O'Dwyer, E. (2017). Hotspots vs. harmspots: Shifting the focus from counts to harm in the criminology of place. *Applied Geography, 86*, 226–244.

Weisburd, D. (2012). Bringing social context back into the equation: The importance of social characteristics of places in the prevention of crime. *Criminology and Public Policy, 11*(2), 317–326. https://doi.org/10.1111/j.1745-9133.2012.00810.x.

Weisburd, D. (2015). The law of crime concentration and the criminology of place. *Criminology, 53*(2), 133–157.

Weisburd, D. (2016). Does hot spots policing inevitably lead to unfair and abusive police practices, or can we maximize both fairness and effectiveness in the new proactive policing? *University of Chicago Legal Forum, 16*, 661–689.

Weisburd, D., Braga, A. A., Groff, E. R., & Wooditch, A. (2017). Can hot spots policing reduce crime in urban areas? An agent-based simulation. *Criminology, 55*(1), 137–173.

Weisburd, D., Bushway, S., Lum, C., & Yang, S. M. (2004). Trajectories of crime at places: A longitudinal study of street segments in the city of Seattle. *Criminology, 42*(2), 283–321.

Weisburd, D. L., Cave, B., Nelson, M., White, C., Haviland, A., Ready, J., Lawton, B., & Sikkema, K. (2018). Mean streets and mental health: Depression and post-traumatic stress disorder at crime hot spots. *American Journal of Community Psychology, 61*, 285–295.

Weisburd, D., Davis, M., & Gill, C. (2015a). Increasing collective efficacy and social capital at crime hot spots: New crime control tools for police. *Policing: A Journal of Policy and Practice, 9*(3), 265–274. https://doi.org/10.1093/police/pav019.

Weisburd, D. L., Eck, J. E., Braga, A. A., Telep, C. W., Cave, B., Bowers, K., Bruinsma, G., Gill, C., Groff, E. R., Hibdon, J., Hinkle, J. C., Johnson, S. D., Lawton, B., Lum, C., Ratcliffe, J. H., Rengert, G., Taniguchi T., & Yang, S. M. (2016a). *Place Matters: Criminology for the Twenty-First Century*. Cambridge: Cambridge University Press.

Weisburd, D., Gill, C., Wooditch, A., Barritt, W., & Murphy, J. (2021a). Building collective action at crime hot spots: Findings from a randomized field experiment. *Journal of Experimental Criminology, 17*(1), 161–191.

Weisburd, D., & Green, L. (1994). Defining the drug market: The case of the Jersey City DMA system. In D. L. MacKenzie and C. D. Uchida (eds.), Drugs and Crime: Evaluating Public Policy Initiatives. Newbury Park, CA: Sage.

Weisburd, D., & Green, L. (1995). Policing drug hot spots: The Jersey City DMA experiment. *Justice Quarterly, 12*, 711–736.

Weisburd, D., Groff, E., & Yang, S. M. (2012). *The Criminology of Place*: *Street Segments and Our Understanding of the Crime Problem*. Oxford: Oxford University Press.

Weisburd, D., Groff, E. R., & Yang, S.-M. (2014a). Understanding and controlling hot spots of crime: The importance of formal and informal social controls. *Prevention Science, 15*(1), 31–43. https://doi.org/10.1007/s11121-012-0351-9.

Weisburd, D., Groff, E. R., Jones, G., Cave, B., Amendola, K. L., Yang, S. M., & Emison, R. F. (2015b). The Dallas patrol management experiment: Can AVL technologies be used to harness unallocated patrol time for crime prevention? *Journal of Experimental Criminology, 11*, 367–391.

Weisburd, D., Lawton, B., Ready, J., & Haviland, A. (2011). *Longitudinal Study of Community Health and Anti-social Behavior at Drug Hot Spots: Details of Methodology*. North Bethesda, MD: National Institute of Drug Abuse of the National Institutes of Health [Grant No. 5R01DA032639–03, 2012]. https://cebcp.org/wp-content/uploads/2020/07/NIDA-Methodology.pdf

Weisburd, D., Maher, L., & Sherman, L. (1992). Contrasting crime general and crime specific theory: The case of hot spots of crime. In F. Adler and W. Laufer (eds.), *New Directions in Criminological Theory*. Advances in Criminological Theory, vol. 4. New Brunswick, NJ: Transaction Press, 45–69.

Weisburd, D., & Majmundar, M. K. (eds.) (2018). *Proactive Policing*: *Effects on Crime and Communities*. Washington, DC: National Academies Press. https://nap.nationalacademies.org/read/24928/chapter/1 (accessed September 11, 2024).

Weisburd, D., Mastrofski, S., McNally, A., Greenspan, R., & Willis, J. (2003). Reforming to preserve: Compstat and strategic problem solving in American policing. *Criminology and Public Policy, 2*, 421–457.

Weisburd, D., Telep, C., & Lawton, B. (2014b). Could innovations in policing have contributed to the New York City crime drop even in a period of declining police strength? The case of stop, question and frisk as a hot spots policing strategy. *Justice Quarterly, 31*(1), 129–153.

Weisburd, D., Telep, C., Vovak, H., Zastrow, T., Braga, A., & Turchan, B. (2022). Reforming the police through procedural justice training: A multi city randomized trial at crime hot spots. *Proceedings of the National Academy of Sciences, 119*(14), 1–6.

Weisburd, D., Petersen, K., & Fay, S. (2023a). Does scientific evidence support the widespread use of SQFs as a proactive police strategy? *Policing: A Journal of Policy and Practice, 17*(1), paac098. https://doi.org/10.1093/police/paac098.

Weisburd, D., Uding, C. V., Hinkle, J. C., & Kuen, K. (2023b). Broken windows and community social control: Evidence from a study of street segments. *Journal of Research in Crime and Delinquency*, *61*(5), 727–771. https://doi.org/10.1177/00224278231168614.

Weisburd, D., & White, C. (2019). Hot spots of crime are not just hot spots of crime: Examining health outcomes at street segments. *Journal of Contemporary Criminal Justice*, *35*(2), 142–160. https://doi.org/10.1177/1043986219832132.

Weisburd, D., White, C., & Wooditch, A. (2020). Does collective efficacy matter at the micro geographic level? Findings from a study of street segments. *British Journal of Criminology*, *60*(4), 873–891.

Weisburd, D., White, C., Wire, S., & Wilson, D. B. (2021b). Enhancing informal social controls to reduce crime: Evidence from a study of crime hot spots. *Prevention Science*, *22*, 509–522. https://doi.org/10.1007/s11121-020-01194-4.

Weisburd, D., Wooditch, A., Weisburd, S., & Yang, S.-M. (2016b). Do stop, question, and frisk practices deter crime? Evidence at micro units of space and time. *Criminology and Public Policy*, 15(1), 31–56.

Weisburd, D., Wyckoff, L., Ready, J., Eck, J., Hinkle, J., & Gajewski, F. (2006). Does crime just move around the corner? A controlled study of spatial displacement and diffusion of crime control benefits. *Criminology*, *44*, 549–592.

Weisburd, D., Zastrow, T., Kuen, K., & Andresen, M. (2024). Crime concentrations at micro places: A review of the evidence. *Aggression and Violent Behavior*, *78*, 101979. https://doi.org/10.1016/j.avb.2024.101979.

Weisheit, R. A., Falcone, D. N., & Wells, L. E. (2006). *Crime and Policing in Rural and Small-Town America*, 3rd ed. Long Grove, IL: Waveland Press.

Wells, L. E., & Weisheit, R. A. (2004). Patterns of rural and urban crime: A county-level comparison. *Criminal Justice Review*, *29*(1), 1–22. https://doi.org/10.1177/073401680402900103.

Wheeler, A., Worden, R., & McLean, S. (2016). Replicating group-based trajectory models of crime at micro-places in Albany, NY. *Journal of Quantitative Criminology*, *32*, 589–612.

Wheeler, A. P., Kim, D.-Y., & Phillips, S. W. (2018). The effect of housing demolitions on crime in Buffalo, New York. *Journal of Research in Crime and Delinquency*, *55*(3), 390–424.

White, M., & Fradella, H. (2016). *Stop and Frisk: The Use and Abuse of a Controversial Policing Tactic*. New York: New York University Press.

White, C., Goldberg, V., Hibdon, J., & Weisburd, D. (2019). Understanding the role of service providers, land use, and resident characteristics on the occurrence of mental health crisis calls to the police. *Journal of Community Psychology, 47*(8), 1961–1982.

White, C., & Weisburd, D. (2018). A co-responder model for policing mental health problems at crime hot spots: Findings from a pilot project. *Policing: A Journal of Policy and Practice, 12*, 194–209. https://doi.org/10.1093/police/pax010.

Wicker, A. W. (1987). Behavior settings reconsidered: Temporal stages, resources, internal dynamics, context. In D. Stokols and I. Altman (eds.), *Handbook of Environmental Psychology*. New York: Wiley & Sons, 613–653.

Wilcox, P., & Eck, J. E. (2011). Criminology of the unpopular: Implications for policy aimed at payday lending facilities. *Criminology and Public Policy, 10* (2), 473–482.

Willis, J. J. (2016). The romance of police pracademics. *Policing: A Journal of Policy and Practice, 10*(3), 315–321.

Wo, J. C. (2023). Crime generators or social capital organizations? Examining the effects of places of worship on neighborhood crime. *PLoS One, 18*(3), e0282196. https://doi.org/10.1371/journal.pone.0282196.

World Bank. (n.d.). Rural population. https://data.worldbank.org/indicator/SP .RUR.TOTL (accessed September 11, 2024).

Wuschke, K., Andresen, M. A., & Brantingham, P. L. (2021). Pathways of crime: Measuring crime concentration along urban roadways. *Canadian Geographies, 65*(3), 267–280.

Zaatut A. (2016). *Social institutions, acculturation, and delinquency risk: A study of second-generation Arab immigrants in an ethnic enclave community*. Unpublished doctoral dissertation, Rutgers University.

Zaatut, A., & DiPietro, S. M. (2023). Revitalizing ethnographic studies of immigration and crime. *Annual Review of Criminology, 6*, 285–306.

Zaatut, A., & Jacobsen, S. K. (2023). Fear among the feared: Arab Americans' fear of crime in an ethnic enclave community. *Crime and Delinquency, 69*(3), 630–655.

Zajacova, A., & Dowd, J. B. (2011). Reliability of self-rated health in US adults. *American Journal of Epidemiology, 174*(8), 977–983.

Zhang, W., Chen, Q., McCubbin, H., McHubbin, L., & Foley, S. (2011). Predictors of mental and physical health: Individual and neighborhood levels of education, social well-being, and ethnicity. *Health and Place, 17*(1), 238–247.

Zidar, M. S., Shafer, J. G., & Eck, J. E. (2018). Reframing an obvious police problem: Discovery, analysis and response to a manufactured problem in a small city. *Policing: A Journal of Policy and Practice, 12*(3), 316–331.

Zimring, F. E. (2012). *The City That Became Safe*. New York: Oxford University Press.

Zoorob, M., & O'Brien, D. T. (2023). *Pacifying problem places: How problem property interventions increase guardianship and reduce disorder and crime*. Unpublished paper, Northeastern University.

# Acknowledgments

Authorship is arranged alphabetically except in the case of David Weisburd, who served as the editor of this Element. We want to thank the Institute of Criminology of the Hebrew University of Jerusalem for its support of the symposium at Kibbutz HaGoshrim (Israel), which allowed for discussion and development of the contributions included. This symposium was part of a broader event in honor of David Weisburd's transition to Emeritus status at the Hebrew University.

# Cambridge Elements ☰

# Criminology

## David Weisburd
*George Mason University, Virginia*
*Hebrew University of Jerusalem*

## Advisory Board

## About the Series

Elements in Criminology seeks to identify key contributions in theory and empirical research that help to identify, enable, and stake out advances in contemporary criminology. The series focuses on radical new ways of understanding and framing criminology, whether of place, communities, persons, or situations. The relevance of criminology for preventing and controlling crime is also be a key focus of this series.

# Cambridge Elements ☰

## Criminology

Printed in the United States
by Baker & Taylor Publisher Services